Resource Books fo

series editor Alan M

Advanced Learners

Alan Maley

OXFORD

UNIVERSITY PRESS

OXFORD
UNIVERSITY PRESS

Great Clarendon Street, Oxford OX2 6DP

Oxford University Press is a department of the University of Oxford.
It furthers the University's objective of excellence in research, scholarship,
and education by publishing worldwide in

Oxford New York

Auckland Cape Town Dar es Salaam Hong Kong Karachi
Kuala Lumpur Madrid Melbourne Mexico City Nairobi
New Delhi Shanghai Taipei Toronto

With offices in

Argentina Austria Brazil Chile Czech Republic France Greece
Guatemala Hungary Italy Japan Poland Portugal Singapore
South Korea Switzerland Thailand Turkey Ukraine Vietnam

OXFORD and OXFORD ENGLISH are registered trade marks of
Oxford University Press in the UK and in certain other countries

First published 2009

2013 2012 2011 2010 2009
10 9 8 7 6 5 4 3 2 1

ISBN: 978 0 19 442194 2

Printed in Spain by Unigraf S.L.

Acknowledgements

For Jayakaran Mukundan

I wish to thank the following for their help and support, and to the many others who did not wish to be named:

Carmen Aguilera, Asta Akutiutiene, Christian Alfaro, Betsy Arroyave, Aphrodite Bantis, Victoria Bermúdez, Jurgen Burg, Nadia Nahomi Castillo-Cáceres, Beatriz Ceballos, Philip Chan, Teresa Gallete de Cittadino, Marcela Corti, Flora Debora, Zoltan Dornyei, Alan Duff, George Filippas, Céleste Franco, Fu Yu, Dimitri Gelveradi, Françoise Grellet, Volker Haberman, Astero Hatzaidi, Marie Havlickova, Patricia Heilig, David A. Hill, Susan Hillyard, Gerard Hocmard, Huang Xiaotong, Aisha Hussain, Roberto Ingravalle, Michael Johnson, Jane Kanjanaphoomin, Bong-Gyu Kim, Sandra Kotzor, Magdalena Kubanyiova, Lee Su Kim, Li Bai, Li Wei, Lin Li Hua, Huyhn thi Kim Lintz, Liu Jun, Nguyen Nhu Anh Loan, Christine Manara, Maria Natalia Maer, Hitomi Masuhara, Peter Medgyes, Alice Méndez, Lucia Militello, Adriana Mitsukami, Zarina Mustapha, Petra Neumeier, Ryo Nitta, Meedy Nugraha, Lily Reyes, Silvia Ruiz, Svetlana Obenansova, Carolina Pansini, Le thi Quynh Chi, Luke Prodromou, Julia Sallabank, José Luis Sánchez-García, Javier Alonso Sánchez-Pinilla, Vyrna Santoso, Inés Sapelli, Dwi Setiawan, Olga Shumilova, Dulip Singh, Kari Smith, Sun Yingying, Janpha Thadphoothon, Mary Thomas, Tan Bee Tin, Brian Tomlinson, Christianne Tosta-Cardoso, Maria Triantafullidou, Penny Ur, Augute Vaiciuliene, Bruno Vilches, Frank Weyhmueller, Xu Zhenghui, Ann Yan, Liliek Yuarono, Adriano Zanetti.

I would also like to thank Helen Forrest, Project Manager of the *Resource Books for Teachers* series, and Natasha Forrest, Senior Production Editor, for their care in seeing this book through to publication. My special thanks go to Ann Hunter for her thoughtful comments, creative suggestions, and meticulous care in editing the manuscript.

The authors and publishers are grateful to those who have given permission to reproduce the following extracts and adaptations of copyright material:

p 32 *Oxford Collocations Dictionary* (OUP, 2009) © Oxford University Press 2009. Used with permission

p 34 Extract from *What is this thing called language* by David Nunan; 2007. Reproduced by permission of Palgrave Macmillan publishers © Palgrave Macmillan 2007.

pp 51 and 91 Extracts from *He knows too much* by Alan Maley; 1999. Reproduced by permission of Cambridge University Press.

p 59 Extract from *The Varieties of Religious Experience* by William James; pp 170–171; 1902. Reproduced by kind permission of Taylor and Francis Group.

pp 67 and 77 Extract from *The Human Zoo* by Desmond Morris, published by Jonathan Cape. Reproduced by permission of The Random House Group Ltd.

p 83 Extracts from *Ladies Coupe* by Anita Nair, published by Chatto & Windus. Reproduced by permission of The Random House Group Ltd.

p 103 Extract from *Musical Cheers and Other Very Short Stories* by Alan Maley (Penguin Books 1997). Text Copyright © Alan Maley, 1997.

p 71 Extract from *Jane Eyre* by Charlotte Brontë, edited by Evelyn Atwell © Longman Publishers 1978. Reproduced by kind permission of Pearson Education Limited.

p 71 Extract from pp 96–7 of *Jane Eyre*, The Oxford Bookworms Library. Text adapted by Clare West © Oxford University Press 2008. Reproduced with permission.

p 74 Extract from *Moth Smoke* by Mohsin Hamid, published by Granta Books. Reproduced by permission of Granta Books.

Although every effort has been made to trace and contact copyright holders before publication, this has not been possible in some cases. We apologize for any apparent infringement of copyright and if notified, the publisher will be pleased to rectify any errors or omissions at the earliest opportunity.

Sources:
p 84 'Darkness Looms' by Nigel Lawson from *Time* Magazine February 2008.

Contents

	Activity	Level	Time (minutes)	Aims	

The author and series editor

Alan Maley worked for the British Council from 1966 to 1988, serving as English Language Officer in Yugoslavia, Ghana, Italy, France, and China, and as Regional Representative in South India (Madras). From 1988 to 1993, he was Director-General of the Bell Educational Trust, Cambridge. From 1993 to 1998 he was Senior Fellow in the Department of English Language and Literature of the National University of Singapore, and from 1998 to 2003 he was Director of the graduate programme at Assumption University, Bangkok. He is currently a freelance consultant. Among his publications are *Literature* (in this series), *Beyond Words*, *Sounds Interesting*, *Sounds Intriguing*, *Words*, *Variations on a Theme*, and *Drama Techniques in Language Learning* (all with Alan Duff), *The Mind's Eye* (with Françoise Grellet and Alan Duff), *Learning to Listen*, and *Poem into Poem* (with Sandra Moulding), *Short and Sweet*, and *The Language Teacher's Voice*.

Foreword

Many language learners reach a relatively comfortable plateau of competence in English, where they can do most of what they need in the language, so they stop developing further. This book is not for them.

There are others however, who although perhaps highly competent in English, are acutely aware of their blind spots, and are constantly trying to achieve higher levels of competence. This book is for them.

As English becomes the language of global interaction and communication, the demand for ever higher levels of competence increases correspondingly. Career opportunities are becoming dependent on a better-than-average level of competence in English. 'Getting by' is no longer an option. In addition, English is becoming a near-essential factor in international social interaction, too.

This book then, is intended for those who have already reached a high level of competence in English but who want or need to go higher still. The assumption is that such learners will be self-motivated, independent, and determined. The activities are therefore demanding in terms of self-investment and effort. At this level there are no quick fixes.

Such students are likely to have highly specific individual requirements. This makes class teaching problematic for some of them. Many of them will prefer to work on a one-to-one basis or to work independently, possibly with a 'study buddy'. The activities in this book are designed in such a way that most of them can be used with small class groups, in one-to-one mode, or by those studying independently. Even students working in a class group will need to do a lot of work outside class. In this respect the book will be of special value to the independent learner.

It is hoped that this book will start a movement to offer truly advanced learners materials which are more appropriate to their level and their aspirations. So-called 'native speakers' might also derive benefit from it!

Alan Maley

Introduction

Why advanced learners?

There are three main reasons why a book of this kind is needed:

1 There is a wealth of published materials for other levels; Beginners, Elementary, Lower-Intermediate, Intermediate, Upper-Intermediate, and Young Learners. There is really very little for advanced students.

2 This still leaves the question 'why'? Surely there are not that many advanced learners around, and most of them are well able to take care of themselves? In fact, with the global spread of English into new geographical areas and professional domains, the demand for higher-level proficiency is rising rapidly. The numbers of advanced learners can be expected to rise, as can the levels of proficiency demanded of them. As Graddol (2006) has pointed out, a merely passable functional command of English will soon no longer be seen as enough. It will be a 'given'—a necessary part of many people's portfolio. So 'getting by in English' will not be sufficient. A far higher level of proficiency will be required.

3 Though advanced learners are, by definition, those who have come a long way in the language, and have a degree of self-sufficiency, they are typically acutely aware of a margin for further improvement. The results of a survey I conducted among over 200 advanced users of English worldwide indicated a demand among highly proficient users of English for something to take them beyond their current levels. Advanced learners, although they may easily out-perform native speakers in many areas, are also well aware of their own blind spots, and are far from complacent about them.

What is an advanced learner?

Unfortunately there is no generally agreed definition of what 'advanced' means. The survey referred to above revealed a bewildering variety of criteria. It seemed best therefore to adopt a 'family resemblance' approach, whereby advanced learners might share some but not all of any of the following characteristics.

1 Definition by occupational demands

This would include people whose occupations require a higher than average command of English: teachers of English, middle and higher management in companies involved in international business, academics from all disciplines who need to interact with peers across the globe, scientific research workers, newly-arrived immigrants to English-speaking countries seeking better employment prospects, and officials in international agencies such as the UN and NGOs. Retired professionals would also qualify for inclusion as the trend toward a longer and more active retirement continues.

Although most of these categories may have a high level of proficiency already, they often find that their jobs steer them into repetitive routines, so that demand for a full range of competencies slackens and they lose some of their initial linguistic 'muscle tone'. This is particularly the case with teachers, who are daily exposed to the often defective English of their students, and who operate well below their own linguistic capacity.

2 Definition by qualifications

No single paper qualification gives a fully adequate measure of high levels of competence. However, we must assume that English users with any of the following fall towards the top of the range: a degree in English as a major subject from a reputable university, UCLES certificates such as CAE, CPE, BEC Higher, a minimum 6.5 on the IELTS scale, or levels C1 or C2 in the Common European Framework.

The list is intended to be indicative, not exclusive. It is clear however, that for the purposes of this book, we are not concerned with students with qualifications much below those indicated.

3 Definition by psychological profile

Advanced learners would, in addition to high proficiency in English, usually also share some of the following characteristics. They would be unusually:

- confident in their ability to improve
- highly motivated, intrinsically and/or extrinsically
- willing to invest in time and energy—to go the extra mile
- willing to take risks with the language
- independent as learners, with strong learning-style preferences
- aware of their weaknesses and areas for improvement
- have high aspirations.

Clearly, lower-level students might also be expected to have some or all of these characteristics but for advanced learners they are essential indicators of success.

The aim of the book then is to stretch learners in two ways:

1 To induct them into things they may not have done before (e.g. writing a poem, teaching a grammar lesson, interviewing a real celebrity).

2 To help them do things they are familiar with to a higher level of proficiency (e.g. making a presentation, writing a formal letter, learning new vocabulary).

Logistic issues

One of the major issues with advanced learners is their learning modes. Many advanced learners are unable or unwilling to attend regular classes, preferring to work alone or one-to-one with a teacher. The survey I conducted showed that preferences were fairly evenly divided between working in a small class group, working one-to-one with a teacher, and studying independently without a teacher.

There are very few books which cater for the needs of individual learners. I have therefore tried to suggest ways in which those working without a teacher can adapt the activities to their own situation. These suggestions can be found in the last item in the Comments section of those activities suitable for such learners.

Whatever the mode, learners will be expected to become autonomous, to take active charge of their own learning. At advanced level above all others, learners are not so much taught as shown how to learn.

The role of the teacher (if there is a teacher) will be as organizer and monitor of the activities. I would suggest too that teachers have a lot to gain by engaging in the activities themselves as co-participants rather than as uninvolved bystanders. Even native speakers will find some of the activities demanding, and there is always something new to discover about language, even when it is your own!

In designing the activities for this book, I have tried to cater to all three modes, though clearly there are some activities which can only be done in groups. Suggestions for each mode are given in the Comments to the activities.

The activities I have offered in this book are by no means comprehensive. In keeping with the principles of the series, I hope that they will spark off new ideas from those who use them. You will certainly find new ways of adapting these activities and of creating others I have not even dreamt of. If you would like to share your ideas, please do so on the OUP website at www.oup.com/elt/teacher/rbt.

How to use this book

The activities are set out as in other books in this series, with some minor variations. Whether you are a teacher selecting activities for your small class or your one-to-one student, or an independent student looking for tasks for yourself, I recommend that you start by carrying out the activities in Chapter 1, 'Getting started.' This will help you decide which other parts of the book to concentrate on first. You can then pick and choose, mix and match to suit your sense of what you and your students need first or most.

Though the chapters are clearly labelled, there will obviously sometimes be overlap between activities in different chapters.

The headings for each activity are as follows:

Level: Although all learners using the materials are assumed to be at a high level, I have sometimes indicated three levels within this as a rough guide to how demanding the activity is:

- High advanced
- Medium advanced
- Basic advanced.

It remains true, of course, that even a very simple activity can be carried out at a very high level, so these levels are no more than an indication of the intrinsic difficulty of an activity.

Time: This is notoriously difficult to predict, especially at advanced level, where learners may become engrossed in a particular activity and carry it well beyond the bounds of what is suggested. And some activities are ongoing; they have no necessary end-point. Nonetheless, I have given suggested timings where they seemed helpful.

Aims: A concise statement of the linguistic, pedagogic, and/or personal development objectives of the activity.

Preparation: A description of any actions or materials needed for the activity.

Procedure: A step-by-step description of what to do when carrying out the activity.

Variations: Suggestions for slightly different ways of doing the activity, or of other related activities.

Follow-up: Any further activities which might reinforce or further develop the activity.

Comments: Points to look out for, advice on possible pitfalls and suggestions for mode of use (see above).

1
Getting started

The purpose of this section of the book is to help you and your learners orientate themselves to what it means to be an advanced learner and how best to organize their work. Apart from the first activity—a SWOT analysis—all the other activities are ways to develop long-term habits which will favour a steady improvement in proficiency in English. It is well known that, beyond a certain point, it becomes more and more difficult to make progress or to notice incremental improvements. Yet by setting clear goals and deadlines, by documenting progress through journals, by developing productive, personally effective study routines, by reinforcing revision techniques and the reading habit, and by making the best use of all the resources available—from websites to reference materials to other people, learners have a better chance of inching ahead. None of these offers spectacular, dramatic change. At this level you cannot expect everything to be bells and whistles either. When you are near the summit, the climb can be slow, but you can still get there!

1.1 SWOT analysis of your own English

Level All levels

Time 60 minutes, repeated later (optional)

Aims To help students focus attention on their strengths and weaknesses in English; to analyse the opportunities/threats they pose; to decide on priorities for action.

Procedure

1 Explain what a SWOT analysis is—essentially a brainstormed list of strengths, weaknesses, opportunities, and threats.

2 Give examples of how this might be applied to competence in English.

Example **Strengths**

- I can read an English newspaper easily.
- I can watch/listen to a feature film in English and understand almost all of what is said.
- I can make casual conversation with other non-native speakers in English with no problems.

Weaknesses

- I find writing a report in English very difficult.
- My pronunciation is sometimes not quite clear.
- I cannot understand some accents in English.

Opportunities

- I could do some extra work on my writing skills.
- I could ask a native speaker to help me with my pronunciation.
- I could spend some time listening to regional accents in English.

Threats

- Writing anything in English frightens me.
- I am embarrassed to start a conversation because of my accent.
- When groups of people are talking together in different accents, I feel inadequate, so I avoid joining in.

3 Ask students to spend about 30 minutes compiling their own SWOT analyses. Then collect them in.

4 Before the next class, analyse the SWOT sheets to see whether there are some common features. This should help determine which sections of the book might be a good place to start. Discuss your conclusions with the group in the next class.

Variation 1

You may prefer to provide students with a list of possible items for each category, to which they then simply respond. These could be based on the lists devised for the Common European Framework in Keith Morrow, *Insights from the Common European Framework*.

Variation 2

An alternative procedure would be to conduct the analysis as a group discussion. This would have the objective of establishing shared SWOT items. This might be more suitable with basic advanced level groups.

Follow-up

Students keep the sheets as a record of their starting point. From time to time, refer back to them, in class or individually, to check on progress. Are there items to add to the *Strengths*, or to remove from the *Weaknesses*?

Comments

1 Thinking in a focused and objective way about how good we are at something, and where we can still improve, is a useful activity in itself. Returning to the SWOT sheets periodically serves to sharpen our self-critical faculties, and helps us to 'keep our eyes on the ball'.

2 If you are working independently, it is still worth starting out with this activity. It will give you a reference point from which you can decide where to start, and to which you can return to review your progress.

1.2 Setting goals and deadlines

Level All levels

Time 60 minutes, followed by regular updating

Aims To provide an objective for students to aim for in the short-, medium-, and long-term; to set realistic time targets for their completion.

Procedure

1 Conduct a brief discussion (10–15 minutes) with students about the value of setting objectives and deadlines for their completion. How many of them already do this in connection with their own occupations? Does the activity have value even if the objectives are not always achieved? How often should we plan to monitor progress towards goals?

2 Individually, students then decide on a set of headings under which they will define their objectives and assign time frames for their completion. Headings might include:

- Speaking skills
- Listening skills
- Reading skills
- Writing skills
- Fluency
- Grammatical accuracy
- Vocabulary growth
- Translation skills
- Interpersonal conversational skills
- Referencing/information-gathering skills
- Media comprehension/interpretation, etc.

3 Check around the group to see what kinds of headings they have chosen.

4 Each student then spends about 20 minutes setting down their own objectives—short-term (by the end of the next week), medium-term (by the end of a month), and long-term (one year from now) for just one of their headings.

5 Collect their sheets for analysis before the next class. Check their objectives for clarity and feasibility before you hand them back next time.

Variation 1

To save time, you can provide the headings for your basic level students and ask them simply to complete their objectives.

Variation 2

Write some of the headings on the board and elicit suggestions from the whole group about feasible objectives for the short, medium, and long term.

Follow-up

1 As homework, ask students to complete their objectives sheet, listing the three most important headings for them. These can then be discussed in the next class. Are they reasonable objectives? Are the time-scales realistic?

2 After the first week, conduct a monitoring session, either individually or with the group as a whole. How far were the first week's objectives achieved? What changes do they need to make for the next week's plan?

Comments

1 We often set ourselves unrealistic targets which we then fail to reach. It is important not to be discouraged by what looks like failure. Tomorrow is another day! We need to develop the habit of constantly revising our deadlines. Making a new list every day is a way of remaining focused on our objectives.

2 If you are working independently or in a one-to-one situation, you can still do this activity for yourself.

1.3 Study routines

Level All levels

Time 30 minutes

Aims To raise students' awareness of the importance of feeling comfortable with their own preferred working style.

Procedure

1 Conduct a 10-minute discussion about the personal aspects of study. You might use the following as a checklist of prompts:

- *When is your best time of day for studying? When are you most alert? When is your energy peak?*
- *How long is your ideal attention span? Do you take regular breaks from study? What do you do during your breaks? How long are your breaks? How do you get yourself back to work again?*
- *Where do you feel most comfortable studying? Do you like to have a 'learning nest' with your favourite objects, pictures, books, etc. around you? Do you have a favourite chair? Do you like to work at a bare table or one loaded with papers? Do you like to play music or do you prefer total silence? What about lighting and ventilation?*
- *Do you have everything you need for study within easy reach—your books, paper, pens, radio/cassette/CD/MP3 player?*
- *Do you like to be in contact with a fellow student or others who might offer support or advice through email, telephone, etc?*

2 Students work in pairs and compare their study preferences. What can they learn from other people's routines?

Follow-up

For the coming week, ask students to be more conscious of the environment in which they work and the routines they follow. Are there ways, even small ways, in which they can improve their study environment (by rearranging the furniture, changing the lighting, letting in fresh air, changing the kind of paper or pen they use, changing the time of day they study, the frequency or length of breaks)?

Comments

1 These may seem trivial matters but, in fact, they are profoundly important. As far as possible, we all need to have an optimal environment which suits our personal preferences in order to function in the most efficient way we can.

2 If you are working independently, not in a class, you can still work on these ideas.

1.4 Keeping a study journal

Level All levels

Time 30 minutes to set up, then ongoing

Aims To persuade students of the value of keeping track of their progress through a study journal or log.

Preparation

Ask students to bring a new, blank notebook to class.

Procedure

1 Briefly discuss the benefits of keeping a study journal in which students record details of what they have done, any problems they encountered, and successes achieved.

2 Suggest ways in which they can organize their journals. Here is one possible way:
   - Decide on the headings, such as *Reading, Writing, Listening, Speaking, Pronunciation, Reference materials used*.
   - Divide the notebook into an equal number of sections: *Reading* pp. 1–15, *Pronunciation* pp. 16–30, etc.
   - For each date reference, use these headings:
     What I did   Problems/successes   What next?

Example **Reading**

20 November

What I did

Read Chapter 1 of Daniel Goleman's *Social Intelligence* (13 pages).

Problems/successes

Was able to read it without using the dictionary. Quite an easy style but some specialist words. Took about an hour.

What next?

Read two more chapters this week. Better make some notes next time though. Try to speed up. Must get hold of his *Emotional Intelligence* book, too.

Follow-up

1 Periodically collect the journals to monitor progress and note any problems mentioned.

2 About once a month, review the journals in a class feedback session.

3 If you are working independently (and even if you are not) take some time at the end of every week to look back over your journal and evaluate what you have done.

Comments

1 It is all too easy to forget what we have done unless we keep a record of it. The journal serves to remind us of the progress we have made and helps us to identify problem areas.

2 Entries do not need to be long or elaborate, so they take up very little time. It is just a question of getting into the habit of doing it regularly.

1.5 Keeping a language notebook/file

Level All levels

Time 30 minutes to present the idea, then ongoing

Aims To help students develop the habit of 'noticing' things about English; to record observations.

Preparation

Ask students to bring a new, blank notebook to class.

Procedure

1 Conduct a brief discussion with students on things they may have noticed recently about English. The kind of things often mentioned include idioms, new words, unusual accents, 'mistakes' made by television announcers, politicians, etc., differences in spelling between UK/US English, colloquial phrases not understood, advertising jingles and slogans, witty shop signs, ambiguity, irony, humour, graffiti, etc. Explain that a healthy curiosity about the language can be one way of extending their range in it. Before we can learn, we often need to notice.

2 Ask students to start a notebook in which they note down any aspect of English which they find interesting or puzzling. There is no need to organize the items in any special way, though some students may like to enter items under headings such as *Grammar*, *New vocabulary*, *Idiomatic phrases*, etc.

3 Periodically, collect in their notebooks and select a few really interesting items for discussion in class.

Variation

Allow a two-week period for noting down items. Then devote one class hour to short presentations of items, at least one from every student.

Follow-up

Over a period of time some interesting material will accumulate which could become the focus of a mini-project. Students might be asked to research a particular category, such as neologisms, by consulting a range of reference materials, and then presenting their findings. (See also 1.6, and Chapter 2 'Tools of the trade'.)

Comments

1 Curiosity about the language is a mark of the advanced learner. Why do we say *spick and span, straight and narrow, fast and loose*? What exactly do they mean, and when can we use them? Why do English people use understatement so much—for example, *not too bad* when they mean *good*? These and a host of other observations can help develop an advanced sensitivity to the way the language functions. In many cases they can lead the learner into new avenues of discovery.

2 You may like to consult a free weekly resource on some quirky aspect of English. Each week Dr Ruth Wajnryb writes a one-page online piece. (See 'Useful websites', page 124.)

1.6 Finding good reference materials

Level   All levels

Time   60 minutes

Aims   To remind students of the importance of reference materials; to direct them to sources of reliable reference tools.

Preparation

Collect samples of reference books you have found useful (bilingual and monolingual dictionaries, thesauruses, grammars, books on usage, encyclopedias, pronunciation dictionaries). The more you have available, the better. Set the books up as a display in the classroom.

Procedure

1 Conduct an open discussion with students about the essential role of reference materials, especially at advanced level. Advanced students work on their own for much of the time, so the support provided by reference works is absolutely crucial.

2 Ask about the kinds of reference books they already use—which dictionaries, grammars, etc. How much use do they make of them? Exactly how do they use dictionaries, for example? Do they simply look up unknown words or use the full range of information dictionaries contain? How satisfied are they? Are they aware of the range of such materials now available?

3 Briefly introduce the reference books in the display. Then allow the students to browse through them. Be available to answer questions. Ask them to be on the lookout for anything new to them, or that they might want to get for themselves.

4 At the end of the session, suggest that each student borrows one book and prepares a brief review of it to present to the group in the next class.

Follow-up

As an ongoing assignment, ask students to research new reference materials from publishers' catalogues, reviews, online searches. These can be compiled into a list for the group to access.

Comments

1 It is all too easy to get so used to one or two trusted reference books and to screen out everything else. The value of this activity is in helping students realize how much else there is out there that could help them.

2 It sometimes comes as a surprise that even advanced students are unaware of the huge range of reference materials currently available. It is also surprising to find what limited use they make of even what they know about. The most recent dictionaries and grammars in particular, offer a rich and authoritative source of information about the language, based on computer corpora. It would be a waste not to use this resource.

3 See the list of key reference works currently available in 'Further Reading', page 122.

1.7 Keeping a log of useful websites

Level All levels

Time 30 minutes, then ongoing

Aims To raise students' awareness of the vast number of useful websites; to develop the habit of keeping a record of the most useful ones.

Preparation

1 Make a list of your own favourite language-related websites. Print out one copy per student.

2 Ask students to bring in details of any websites they have found useful in connection with their own study of English.

Procedure

1 Distribute your printed list. Students work in pairs or threes to compare your list with theirs. They should add any websites they think might be interesting to their own lists. Allow 15 minutes for this. (See the possible list in 'Useful websites', page 124.)

2 Discuss students' findings in an open session, asking the group to recommend three really interesting and useful sites they have used.

3 Ask students to continue adding to their lists of useful sites as they discover new ones.

Follow-up

Periodically run a sharing session where students describe new sites they have discovered and report on any sites that have changed or disappeared!

Comments

1 The Internet is an infinite resource. This is its greatest value and also its greatest disadvantage. It is possible to waste enormous amounts of time in futile searches or surfing. This activity helps focus attention on some proven sites and encourages sharing information as well as careful recording and updating.

2 If you are working independently, the Internet can be even more valuable to you as a resource. In your case, check out some of the sites in 'Useful websites', page 124, and continue to add sites as you come across them.

Acknowledgements

I am indebted to Diana Eastment for her regular column in the *ELT Journal* for some of these sources.

1.8 The reading habit

Level All levels

Time 60 minutes, then ongoing

Aims To raise students' awareness of the importance of extensive reading.

Procedure

1 Students discuss with you what they consider the most important ways of learning more language. If reading comes up, fine. If not, raise it at the end, and explain that research has shown that extensive reading—reading rapidly and copiously, with no questions or activities, and where reading is its own reward, is the single most effective way of maintaining the language they know, and of learning more. Allow about one minute for this information.

2 Ask students to work in pairs. Allow 15 minutes for them to brainstorm ways they think would promote the reading habit.

3 At the end, note all the suggestions on the board and discuss their feasibility with the group. Ask them to select two or three of the suggestions (their own or others') which they agree to try out for a month. When the month is up, take time to discuss how effective the strategies have been for each individual.

Variation

With basic advanced-level students, it may be better to supply a list for step 2 above. Ask them in pairs to discuss the list and report back on their preferences. Here are a number of suggestions:

- *Set aside a time every day for reading anything you like—a newspaper, a magazine, a short story, a novel, a commercial, a catalogue. Decide how long you will read: 30 minutes? An hour? More?*
- *Choose something to read that you do not normally read. For example, if you never read short stories, film reviews, or articles about science, try reading some.*
- *Go to a good library or bookshop and browse for an hour. Borrow or buy something which looks really interesting. Then read it!*
- *Subscribe to a weekly newspaper or magazine in English. Read everything in it, even the ads.*
- *Set yourself some reading targets. (See 1.2 'Setting goals and deadlines'.) Decide how many pages you will read every day, or how many books you will read in a month or a year. Monitor yourself.*
- *Try to increase your reading speed. Start to read a new book or article. Stop after three minutes. Make a pencil mark to show where you got to. The next day start reading from the beginning again. Read for three minutes and mark where you have got to this time. Do this for five days and see how much faster you are reading.*

Follow-up

1 Ask students, whatever strategy they use, to keep a careful record of what they read, and any observations about it that occur to them. (See 1.4 'Keeping a study journal'.)

2 Periodically, the group share their reading with each other. What have they found most interesting? Are there books or articles others might like to read? Are there things they would definitely not recommend? (See also Chapter 5 'Focus on reading'.)

Comments

1 Advanced students should aim to join a 'confederacy of readers'—a reading community or group from which they get ideas on what they have read, what else there is to read, and from which they derive strength and motivation based on a shared passion for reading.

2 Anyone interested in the compelling research evidence in support of extended reading should consult Stephen Krashen, *The Power of Reading: Insights from the Research.*

3 If you are working independently, you can and should do this activity, though you will not have the benefit of input from other students. However, you may have other opportunities to share your reading experience, perhaps with email friends, on your blog, socially, or with friends at work.

1.9 Revision techniques

Level All levels

Time 60 minutes, followed by regular monitoring and review

Aims To share effective revision techniques; to develop personal revision strategies.

Procedure

1 Lead off the class with some questions to the group about revision, for example:

- *Do you all revise or review material you have met for the first time?*
- *How often do you revise? For how long?*
- *Do you have any special tricks or techniques for consolidating what you have learnt?*

2 Ask students in pairs to come up with a set of recommendations for revision, including suggested frequency, duration, and techniques. Allow 15 minutes for this.

3 Each pair makes a brief presentation of their recommendations. If possible, list the main points on the board in three columns:

Frequency   Duration   Technique

At the end, try to find agreement under each category through open discussion.

4 As a homework assignment, ask each student to prepare a personal schedule for revision based on the discussion and ideas from the class.

Follow-up

After about a month, conduct a brief feedback session on revision. Ask:

- *How well have you held to your revision schedules?*
- *How well are the revision schedules working?*
- *What changes, if any, do you want to make?*

Comments

1 We rarely, if ever, learn a piece of language after meeting it just once. Repetition lies at the heart of language and of language learning. At this level, students are usually well aware of this. The activity simply serves to remind them of the need for revision and gets them thinking about how best to do it.

2 Many books on study techniques recommend that we revise at longer and longer intervals and for shorter and shorter times. For example, when reviewing vocabulary, the next day do it for 15 minutes, one week later for ten minutes, one month later for five minutes. As to techniques, there are any number of ways to commit things to memory: by repeating them aloud over and over (in the manner of Koranic schools), by rereading a passage, then trying to make notes on it from memory, by keeping vocabulary cards and transferring

them from one pocket to another as they are mastered, by making mind maps, by using mnemonics, and many more. But we also have to remember that we need different strokes for different folks. Students should use techniques they feel comfortable with.

1.10 Using other people as resources

Level All levels

Time 60 minutes, plus follow-up

Aims To raise students' awareness of ways of drawing on the expertise and support of others; to make plans for using this expertise and support.

Procedure

1 Lead an open discussion on the kinds of people who might be able to help students to improve their proficiency in English. Some possible suggestions would be: the teacher (if there is one), fellow students (if working in a group), native speakers of English in the area, expert users of English (such as local university teachers, businessmen, journalists, etc.), fluent English-speaking relatives.

2 Then ask in what ways such people might be asked to help. Some possible ideas: they could be asked to read over written assignments and comment on them, converse informally in English, communicate by email, suggest books or materials, simply lend a friendly ear to problems, or work collaboratively on an assignment.

3 Finally, ask students individually to draw up a list of people they personally could call on for help. For each person they should specify the kind of help they might expect from them. Their assignment is to approach the people they have listed for help.

Variation 1

To save time, you might draw up a list of likely helpers. Ask students to describe the kind of help each might give. Students then decide which of them might help in their individual cases.

Variation 2

Alternatively, begin by asking students what sort of help and support they feel they need. They draw up a list in pairs. Then ask for suggestions about who might be able to provide that help.

Follow-up

Periodically, check whether students have been able to tap into the help they outlined in step 3 above. If not, offer alternative suggestions and practical help as appropriate.

Comments

1 In general, we need others. 'No Man is an Ilande' as the 17th century poet John Donne reminds us. What we need to do is to become more aware of where we might get the help we need.

2 Particularly if you are studying independently, it is critically important that you get as much help and support as you can. You will be surprised at how helpful and supportive people can be if approached in a tactful and sensitive way.

2
Tools of the trade

Reference materials are a priceless resource for advanced learners in particular. It is therefore well worth spending time getting to know them really well. For an aspiring advanced learner, a minimum set of reference materials would include two advanced learner's monolingual dictionaries, a bilingual dictionary, a reference grammar, a thesaurus and, if possible, a dictionary of collocations and an encyclopedia. (See 1.6 'Finding good reference materials' and the sample list in 'Further reading, page 122.) Any school claiming to teach at an advanced level should also be well supplied with sets of such materials. This chapter presents some ideas for familiarizing students with these reference tools so that the best use can be made of them.

2.1 Comparing dictionaries

Level All levels

Time 30 minutes, plus follow-up

Aims To help students become critically aware of the relative merits of two (or more) dictionaries; to develop learner autonomy in the use of dictionaries.

Preparation

1 Make sure there are enough dictionaries available so that each student can consult two different ones. There should be at least two or three monolingual dictionaries among them.

2 Make enough copies of Worksheet 2.1 for one per student.

Procedure

1 Lead a brief discussion about dictionaries and the information they provide. Then ask students to work in pairs to design a checklist of all the kinds of information they would expect to find in a good dictionary. Allow 20 minutes for this, then conduct a brief feedback session to make sure they have not omitted anything important.

2 Distribute two dictionaries to each pair. Ask students to compare them, using their checklists. They should note down how well the dictionaries match up to their key criteria. Ask *What differences have you found? Are they important?*

3 Give out Worksheet 2.1. How does it compare with their own checklists? Invite them to edit their own lists if they notice things they had omitted.

4 For homework, ask students to prepare a brief written report on the two dictionaries they compared in class, using their edited checklists.

Worksheet 2.1

Checklist for comparing dictionaries

1 Are the page layouts, print size, and headings easy to read?
2 Are the instructions for use clear and uncluttered?
3 How many headwords are covered? How many entries are there?
4 Is there a defining vocabulary? How big is it?
5 How clear are the definitions?
6 How helpful are the citations (the quotations)?
7 How much linguistic information is there in each entry? (grammatical information, collocations, fixed phrases, synonyms/equivalents, geographical variety, stylistic labels, historical derivation, frequency, variant spellings, etc.)
8 What other features does the dictionary contain? (grammar boxes, information on common errors, lists of abbreviations, lists of acronyms, lists of proper names, boxes for lexical fields, cultural information, etc.)

Photocopiable © Oxford University Press

Variation

To save time, or with slightly lower-level groups, distribute the checklist first.

Follow-up

1 In a following class, conduct a class discussion on the students' preferred dictionaries, based on their written reports. How much agreement is there?

2 In another follow-up class, divide the class into groups of three. Distribute two or more dictionaries to each group. Write up a list of words, for example, *affective, negate, pitch, squall, alien*. Allow ten minutes for students to consult the entries for these words in their dictionaries. What differences do they note? Then ask for feedback in open discussion. What did students notice?

Comments

1 Dictionaries often appear to be more or less the same. It is only when we start to look at them critically that we notice that there are many differences between them, both in the quantity of information they contain and the way it is presented. David Crystal, in *How Language Works*, reports that large dictionaries can differ by as much as 50 per cent in the information they contain. That is why it is advisable to consult more than one dictionary!

2 Given the importance of dictionaries as reference tools and the reverence with which they are regarded, it is important that advanced learners become very familiar with the strengths and weaknesses of the dictionaries they use. This activity is just one way of developing a critical familiarity with dictionaries.

3 If you are working independently, you almost certainly already have at least one good dictionary. If you have two, or can borrow another one, you can complete the activity on your own.

2.2 The thesaurus

We use a dictionary to look up the meaning of a word we do not know. We use a thesaurus to find the unknown word which best matches a meaning we already know. The most famous thesaurus of all time is the one developed by Peter Mark Roget and published in 1852. This is still going strong in revised editions. One problem with Roget is that, although he gives a large number of words which denote a particular meaning, there is no way for readers to decide which is the most appropriate one for their purposes. Unless you know it already, Roget is not much help. Recent adaptations of the thesaurus idea have given us more helpful ways of identifying just which of the many possible words available is the one we need. In this section, we shall suggest ways of familiarizing students with this highly valuable resource.

Level All levels

Time 2 class hours, plus regular follow-up

Aims To introduce the concept of a thesaurus; to give students practice in using and comparing thesauruses critically.

Preparation

Class 1

1 Make sure you have enough copies of at least two up-to-date thesauruses, such as the *Oxford Thesaurus, Roget's Thesaurus, Longman English Activator, Longman Lexicon of Contemporary English*.

2 Either prepare your own list of synonyms/equivalences or print out enough copies of Worksheet 2.2a for one per student.

Worksheet 2.2a

Words with similar meanings
1 need, require, want, demand, call for
2 advocate, promote, counsel, suggest, tip, guide
3 steal, rob, burgle, pinch, extort, nick, take, lift, shoplift, embezzle, poach, defraud
4 luck, coincidence, fortune, fate, destiny, providence
5 small, tiny, minute, minuscule, microscopic
6 dirty, filthy, grubby, mucky, grimy, dusty, yucky

Photocopiable © Oxford University Press

Procedure

1 Lead a discussion about synonyms. Show how complete synonymy is almost impossible. For example, 'big' and 'large' are not really synonyms. You can speak of *a big laugh* but not of *a large laugh*; likewise with *high* and *tall*. *A tall lady* is possible, but not a *high lady*.

2 Students work in pairs. Distribute two thesauruses to each pair. Give out Worksheet 2.2a. Allow 15 minutes for them to check the differences between at least two of these sets of words, using the thesaurus.

3 Pairs report back. Were there any problems or disagreements?

4 Now ask the same pairs to compare the two thesauruses they have, using these questions as guidelines:

- *How easy is it to understand the directions for using the thesaurus?*
- *How easy is it to find the information you need?*
- *How much additional information does the thesaurus provide (word meanings, collocations)?*

5 Students prepare a brief written report for the next class on the thesauruses they reviewed.

Preparation

Class 2

Print out enough copies of Worksheet 2.2b below for one per three students.

Worksheet 2.2b

	modesty	pride	passport	teeth	illness	exam	diamonds	gun	Tudor
fake									
sham									
false									
mock									

	wind	desire	drug	influence	empire	army	leader	weapon	smell
strong									
potent									
mighty									
powerful									

	a bill	a patient	tax returns	the headlines	a building	a word's meaning	the records	the accounts
check								
inspect								
scrutinize								
examine								
scan								

Photocopiable © Oxford University Press

Procedure

1 Discuss the evaluation reports from the previous class.

2 Lead a discussion on how words differ in shades of meaning. Sometimes these relate to small but key differences in meaning, such as *walk*, *stride*, *amble*. Sometimes they relate to collocation: we can *direct a play*, but we *conduct a series of tests*, we *supervise a student*, and we *run a business*.

3 Students work in groups of three. Distribute Worksheet 2.2b to each group. Ask them to complete the matrices by ticking the boxes which correspond to the most likely collocations (e.g. they can tick *false modesty* but not *fake modesty*). Warn students that for some words they can tick more than one box. If they are in any doubt, they should consult a thesaurus.

4 Allow 20 minutes for this, then conduct class feedback to discuss any disagreements or borderline cases.

Follow-up

Remind students to continue to work on thesauruses. They can also try out free websites which offer information on synonyms and antonyms. (See 'Useful websites', page 125 for suggestions to get them started.)

Comments

1 The differences between words which appear to be similar in meaning can vary in different ways: in terms of different collocations and colligations (see 3.1 'Collocation and colligation'); in terms of specific semantic features—whether an action is one-off or repeated, whether it is fast or slow, whether it has positive or negative connotations, or in terms of register (the difference between *quid* and *pound*). Thesauruses give us access to this type of information about words, hence their importance for advanced learners.

2 At more elementary levels of language learning, it is sufficient to rely heavily on 'core vocabulary' such as *walk*, *talk*, *say*, *tell*, *make*, etc. But at a more advanced level, we need to expand from this core so that speaking and writing become both more expressive and more precise. The thesaurus is an invaluable tool for this, provided the advanced student knows how to use it.

Acknowledgements

The ideas for the matrices have been adapted from Rudzka, *The Words You Need*.

Comments

If you are working independently and have a thesaurus, you can do this activity. If not, try to borrow one from your nearest public library, or buy one.

2.3 Dictionaries of collocations

Level All levels

Time 60 minutes, plus follow-up

Aims To familiarize students with collocations dictionaries; to help students develop a critical appreciation of their value.

Preparation

Make sure you have enough copies of a number of different dictionaries of collocations available.

Procedure

1 Introduce the students to the ideas behind a collocations dictionary. As they know, words rarely occur alone and they tend to prefer the company of some words rather than others. The likelihood of one word being found with others is its frequency of collocation. As a user of English, knowing this is an important part of knowing the word.

2 Work out with the students a brief checklist to help them compare the dictionaries. Write the checklist on the board.

Example **Checklist for comparing dictionaries**
- Are all the words in both dictionaries? (coverage)
- How easy is it to find what you are looking for?
- How much information is given for a word?
- How easy is it to read the entries? (style? layout?)
- Which one do you prefer? Why?

3 Display the collocations dictionaries on a table and let each pair of students choose two dictionaries to work with. Allow them about 30 minutes to compare two or three entries for the same word in the two dictionaries. Here are some suggested words:

commonplace, emotion, moral, succession, timing

4 Check on the results. Which dictionary does the majority of students prefer? Why?

5 As homework, ask students to check three or four other entries and to write up their evaluations, using this additional information.

Variation

Set this activity as a homework assignment. In class you will need to introduce collocations dictionaries, agree on criteria for evaluating them, and distribute the dictionaries. Then give students two weeks to prepare an evaluation report comparing the two dictionaries.

Follow-up

Encourage students to compile their own collocations dictionary by noting the contexts of new words each time they meet them, and entering them alphabetically in a loose leaf folder, so that they can add pages.

2.4 Comparing grammars

Level All levels

Time 60 minutes

Aims To introduce students to the range of pedagogical grammars available; to help students develop a critical attitude towards them.

Preparation

1 Make sure that you have a selection of at least three or four reputable reference grammars available in sufficient numbers for groups of four to have a set each. (See 1.6 'Finding good reference materials' for a list of possible reference grammars.)

2 Print enough copies of Worksheet 2.4 for one per student.

Worksheet 2.4

Checklist for comparing grammars

1 How easy is it to find what you are looking for? Is there a Table of Contents, an Index? Is there cross-referencing?

2 How easy is it to understand what you were looking for once you have found it? For example, is the overall organization of the grammar clear? Is it well indexed and signposted? Is the page layout helpful, or cluttered and confusing? Are the rubrics clear and at the right level of difficulty for you? Is the terminology transparent?

3 Are the rules clearly written, unambiguous, accurate, useful to you as a learner?

4 Are the examples authentic and helpful?

5 Does it distinguish between spoken and written grammar?

6 Does it contain other useful information? For example about frequency of use, register, hints on usage in general?

7 Would you recommend it to a friend?

Procedure

1 Discuss with students what they expect a good grammar reference book to provide. Note the points on the board.

2 After about ten minutes, distribute Worksheet 2.4, one per student. Let them compare it with the points they raised in step 1. They may wish to add some of these to the worksheet list.

3 Working in pairs, they now collect copies of two grammars from the front table and submit them to a comparative examination. One useful way of doing this is to select just one item and compare how it is presented in the two grammars. For example, how do they deal with article usage, with nominalization, or with phrasal verbs? Allow about 30 minutes for this.

4 Check their findings. Set a homework assignment in which they prepare a written evaluation of the two grammars.

Comments

1 It is widely assumed that, just as with dictionaries, if something is in a grammar book, it must be true and authoritative. In fact, grammars differ widely in many respects. This activity is one way of revealing these differences and helping learners to develop discrimination.

2 If you are studying independently, you can do this activity. However, it will involve you buying or borrowing at least two good grammars!

2.5 Encyclopedias

Level All levels

Time 30 minutes, plus follow-up

Aims To familiarize students with sources of information from websites; to encourage them to evaluate these sources critically through comparison.

Preparation

1 Print out a list of some of the more readily accessible online encyclopedias. (See 'Useful websites', page 125.) You may wish to add to the list yourself.

2 Prepare a list of possible topics which might be suitable for your students to research. This will depend on their main areas of interest and cognitive level, so it is a matter for your own discretion and knowledge of your students.

3 Prepare a checklist of points to consider when evaluating an encyclopedia. Print out enough copies of the checklist (Worksheet 2.5) for one per student.

Worksheet 2.5

Checklist for evaluating an encyclopedia

1 How comprehensive is the information? Is there too much? Not enough?
2 How accessible is it in terms of finding the information you want and making sense of it once you have found it?
3 How reliable is the information? Is it consistent with that derived from other sources?
4 How attractive is the layout? Are there illustrations?
5 How much cross-referencing is there to related topics?

Procedure

1 In today's information society there are many ways of finding any information we need. The easiest is to simply consult one of the major search engines like Yahoo or Google. However, there is still something to be said for encyclopedias, which are organized

precisely to offer comprehensive information about almost anything. Explain to the students that they will conduct a piece of Internet research into the quality of information offered by at least two Internet encyclopedia websites.

2 Write up topics available for research. Just as an example, you might decide that 'ancient civilizations' is an appropriate subject area. So you might list these topics on the board:

- The Hittites
- The pre-Columbian civilizations of America
- The Mughal Empire
- The Etruscans
- Minoan Crete
- The Mayan Empire
- The Khmer Empire.

3 Students should choose just one of these.

4 Distribute Worksheet 2.5, one per student. Below are the points on which they will base their comparison. They may wish to add other items. Explain that they will have two weeks in which to:

- Decide which two or three online encyclopedias they will use.
- Carry out a comparison of these information sources, using the checklist.
- Prepare a written report on their evaluation.

5 On the due date, hold an open discussion on their findings, and collect the written evaluations.

Comments

1 This activity ensures that students have a working familiarity with some of the better-known online information resources. They will also have a better appreciation of the reliability and accessibility of such resources. This may well save them precious time later on.

2 If you are working independently, this activity is perfect for you. You will simply need to decide which topic to research.

3

Focus on vocabulary

A large and active vocabulary is a defining feature of a really advanced user of any language. The more words we know, in the sense of being able to use them appropriately, the better and more subtly we are able to communicate our meanings. This chapter will focus on ideas for raising students' awareness of the lexical system, for consolidating vocabulary, and for expanding and extending vocabulary. Some activities, such as 3.4 'Prefixes and suffixes', are designed to tap into the systems of vocabulary. Others relate to the way vocabulary items are linked with others, for example, through collocation and colligation. The main aim is to encourage advanced learners to immerse themselves in the ocean of English words and to learn to swim happily there.

3.1 Collocation and colligation

Level All levels

Time 2 class hours, plus follow-up

Aims To introduce students to the key concepts of lexical collocation and grammatical colligation.

Preparation

1 Make sure that you are familiar with the notions of collocation and colligation. For definitions, please check your favourite dictionary.

2 Print out concordances for one or more words from a computer corpus site. (See 'Useful websites', page 125.)

3 A sample page for the words *spend* and *waste* is printed below and overleaf. Make enough copies for one per pair.

Sample text

> spend
>
> ... that Maggie preferred to **spend** them about the house ...
> ... Council's Negotiating Committee to **spend** several futile days negotiating ...
> ... do not have to **spend** money on peppermints, either ...
> ... reason why the famous **spend** a fortune on this ...
> ... My brother used to **spend** all his free time ...
> ... a girl I'd want to **spend** the rest of my ...

> **waste**
>
> ... T.S. Eliot's poem The **Waste** Land begins a new ...
> ... a new place to dump **waste** by the end of ...
> ... our ceiling from the **waste** outlet of the shower ...
> ... 'My dear, I wouldn't **waste** any sleep,' said Constance ...
> ... Why are you going to **waste** your time there if ...
>   ... that it will be a **waste** of time and money ...

4 Have enough copies of *The Oxford Dictionary of Collocations* and *The Oxford Thesaurus* available. (See also Chapter 2 'Tools of the Trade' for other uses of these reference tools.)

Procedure

1 Hold a brief discussion about collocation and colligation. Explain that words seem to have a special attraction for some other words and not others. When the words are content words, we refer to this as collocation. When they are grammatical words, we call it colligation. Give some examples of both. For example, common collocations of *result* would be *a disappointing result, an unexpected result, a final result*. Common colligations would include *as a result of ...*, *a result which ...*, *the best result was ...* '. Ask for examples of collocations and colligations for some other common words, such as: *fruit, run, take, hand, smile, hope*.

2 Students work in pairs. Distribute the printouts of the concordance lines for *spend* and *waste*, one per pair of students. For each of the two words, they should make a list of the most common collocates and colligations. Collect feedback after 15 minutes. Discuss any unusual collocations.

3 Students work in groups of three. Each group should have either of the two reference resource books available. (See step 4 of Preparation.) Each group selects one word from the following list: *involvement, maintain, public, offer, steady, victim*. Using the reference work they have, they find out as much as possible about the collocates and colligations of their word and note them down.

4 Groups then take turns to report on their findings to the rest of the class.

Follow-up

1 As a homework assignment, ask students to research the collocation information on a number of other words and to report back on this in a future class. They can either consult the British National Corpus website (see 'Useful websites, page 125) or use one of the reference works mentioned in step 4 of Preparation.

2 Ask students to ensure that their vocabulary notebooks always contain information on both collocation and colligation as they add new items.

Comments

1 It is a key part of knowing a word that we know which other words it is most likely to co-occur with. As proficient users of English, we have expectations about which words will keep each other company. If we

use an abnormal collocation, it either reveals our incompetence or our creativity. Poets especially are always upsetting our expectations. Regrettably however, most language learners, even at the advanced level, are not poets.

2　If you are working independently, you can still do the activity. Choose a word that you feel you have trouble working out collocations for. Write down some of your choices and then check them in *The Oxford Dictionary of Collocations*.

3.2　All-purpose vocabulary

Level　All levels

Time　60 minutes, plus regular follow-up

Aims　To raise students' awareness of the usefulness of vocabulary which summarizes in a general word what is referred to elsewhere by more detailed words.

Preparation

1　To practise using some of this type of vocabulary, print out Worksheet 3.2.

2　Make enough copies for one per student.

Worksheet 3.2

1　thing	perspective	structure	response
2　fact	viewpoint	framework	respect
3　factor	view	context	growth
4　issue	point of view	development	
5　problem	approach	possibility	
6　matter	component	basis	potential
7　question	part	technique	
8　case	quality	strategy	
9　aspect	element		
10　instance	area		
11　example	process	field	
12　phenomenon	mechanism	medium	
13　occurrence	operation	situation	
14　characteristic	mode	complex	
15　version	way	nexus	
16　feature	workings	dimension	
17　item	range		
18　situation	effect	type	
19　result	nature		
20　consequence	level		

Photocopiable © Oxford University Press

3　Make copies of one or two short texts containing some of these words.

Sample text 1

> Written and spoken language have their own typical features: for example, written language tends to have a greater percentage of content words to function words than spoken language. However, those features typically associated with written language can appear in spoken language and vice-versa.

David Nunan, *What is this thing called language?*

Sample text 2

> Discussion of energy in Europe today tends to be dominated by what are described as environmental issues, chiefly the question of carbon emissions and global warming. So much so, in fact, that the rather more urgent matter of security of supply is all too often overlooked. But it is now becoming acute. It has two dimensions. The first relates…

Nigel Lawson, *Time magazine*

Procedure

1 Distribute Worksheet 3.2. Ask students to look at it carefully in pairs and try to find what is common to these words.

2 Collect feedback. Students will probably tell you that these are all general nouns. Ask if there are any reasons for grouping them on the worksheet:

- *What do the words in each group have in common?*
- *How common are these words?*

Make sure that students understand that these are all words which can refer back to more detailed information in a text.

3 Distribute the texts you have chosen. Students read and underline the words from Worksheet 3.2 in each (*features, issues, question, matter, dimensions*). Discuss with the students how these words help tie the text together and how they economize effort by acting as a kind of shorthand for more detailed items.

4 Students now choose two of the words from the list in Worksheet 3.2. They write two short paragraphs using each of the two words. The paragraphs do not need to be connected to each other but they may be. Allow 15 minutes for this.

5 In groups of four, students compare their paragraphs. If there is time, discuss some of the paragraphs with the students in full-class feedback.

Follow-up

1 As a homework project, students collect at least three texts which contain some of these words. They should make copies of the texts with the words underlined. Set a date for them to bring their texts to class for further discussion and sharing.

2 As an ongoing project, students add any words they find to the original list you have given them. Here are a few to start with: *debate, inquiry, objection, topic, theme, subject, change, episode.*

Comments

1 Words like these occur so commonly that it is not difficult to find texts which exemplify them. A quick search of almost any newspaper or magazine will provide a rich selection.

2 If you are working independently, you can still follow the Procedure section of this activity, but you will not be able to compare with a fellow student, unless you have found an email 'study-buddy' with similar interests.

3.3 Word formation

Level   All levels

Time   60 minutes, plus follow-up

Aims   To activate students' knowledge of word formation as a generative tool; to give practice in extending word stock through grammatical word changes.

Preparation

1 Prepare some examples of content words which can shape themselves into different parts of speech. For example, *deceive* (v), *deceit* (n), *deceitful* (adj), *deceitfully* (adv). Worksheet 3.3a contains a selection of examples. Notice that the examples given sometimes do not have words for all four parts of speech. Some may have two forms for the same part of speech (e.g. *deceit/deception*). Some may change their meaning in one or more of the parts of speech (e.g. *dissolutely*).

2 Make enough copies of Worksheet 3.3a for one per student.

3 Make sure that there are plenty of dictionaries around for reference and checking purposes.

Procedure

1 Write up one or two examples of 'core' words, either verbs or nouns. For example: *intend, pretend, defend, transcend*. Elicit how these words would change if they functioned as a different part of speech. For example, *defend* (v) can become *defence* or *defender* (n), *defensive* (adj), *defensively* (adv). Work through the other words in the same way. What do students notice? Although these words all have the same ending (*-end*), they sometimes form parts of speech differently. For example, *transcendental* (adj), *pretension* (n), *intentional* (adj).

2 Distribute Worksheet 3.3a, one per student. Students work in pairs. Ask:

- *What do you notice?*
- *Which words change their meanings when they change their form? (revolve/ revolution)*
- *Which slots are unfilled? (the verb for the adjective wise)*
- *Which ones form more than one word in a slot? (alive/living/lively)*

Allow 15 minutes for this, then collect feedback. Students consult their dictionaries as necessary.

3 In groups of three, students then select five content words randomly from one of their dictionaries. The easiest way to do this is to open the dictionary at any page and select the first content word on the left hand page. They do this five times. They then work to generate as many other forms of the word as they can, based on changing the part of speech. Allow about ten minutes for this, then collect feedback, noting interesting cases on the board.

Worksheet 3.3a

Content word forms

Verb	Noun	Adjective	Adverb
deceive	deceit	deceitful	deceitfully
	deception	deceptive	deceptively
conceive	conceit	conceited	conceitedly
conceive	conception	conceptual	conceptually
receive	reception	receptive	receptively
reprieve	reprieve	reprieved	
retrieve	retrieval	retrieved	
relieve	relief	relieved	
believe	belief	belief	
involve	involvement	involved	
resolve	resolution	resolute	resolutely
		resolved	
revolve	revolution	revolted	revoltedly
	revolt	revolving	
dissolve	dissolution	dissolute	dissolutely
solve	solvent		
live	life	lively	
		alive/living	
	baddie	bad	badly
own	owner		
	ownership		
	wisdom	wise	wisely

Photocopiable © Oxford University Press

Variation

Prepare a worksheet with only one slot completed. Students then need to complete the empty slots where possible. Here is a sample of part of such a sheet.

Worksheet 3.3b

Verb	Noun	Adjective	Adverb
fit			
	relief		
		absolute	
			descriptively

Photocopiable © Oxford University Press

Comments

1 An awareness of word formation can be a powerful way to generate new words and thereby to extend vocabulary. Sometimes this can mean four for the price of one. However, it is also necessary to beware! The systems for forming words in this way are complex and often appear illogical. It takes a long time to develop the intuitive 'feel' for words and how they 'sprout' from each other. This can only be developed over time, hence the need for repeated practice in this area.

2 If you are working independently, you can do all these activities provided you have access to a good dictionary. (See also 2.1 'Comparing dictionaries'.)

3.4 Prefixes and suffixes

Level All (but see Comments below)

Time 60 minutes, plus regular follow-up

Aims To raise student's awareness of the meanings of English prefixes and suffixes; to show how prefixes and suffixes can increase comprehension and word-building skills.

Preparation

1 Make a list of the more common prefixes in English, along with their meanings and some examples. (See 'Useful websites', page 125 for a fairly comprehensive list.)

2 Make enough copies of Worksheets 3.4a, 3.4b, 3.4c, and 3.4d for one per student.

3 Now provide the meanings and examples for the following prefixes: *de-, dis-, en-, ex-, extra-, in-, im-, inter-, intra-, non-, out-, over-, post-, pre-, pro-, re-, semi-, sub-, trans-, un-, under-*.

Procedure

1 Find out how much students already know about prefixes. If necessary, explain that they are detachable parts of a word ('morpheme' is the technical term). They can be used to add a new element of meaning to an existing word or to another morpheme. For example, *possible–impossible, mine–undermine*, etc.

2 Distribute Worksheet 3.4a. Students work in pairs. Allow them ten minutes to add as many words as possible to the Examples column (in *a-/an-* they might add *apathetic, aneurism, anorexia*, etc.).

3 Collect examples from the class and note them on the board. Make sure they are examples of real prefixes.

4 Students now work in groups of four to find meanings and examples for the other prefixes listed in Worksheet 3.4a. Allow 15 minutes for this, then collect examples as in step 3 above.

5 It is unlikely students will have found all the possible examples, so ask them to complete their worksheet for homework.

Worksheet 3.4a

Common prefixes

Prefix	Meaning	Example
a-/-an	not/without	anaemic/anathema
		_____
a-	to/towards/around	aside
		_____
ab-	away, from	abstract/abduct
		_____
ad-	change into	addition/advance
		_____
a-/ac-/ag-/af-/al-/an-/ ap-/at-/as-/at-	movement to	affirm/ascend
		_____
anti-	against/opposite	antiseptic/antithesis
		_____
be-	covered with/ completely	besmirched/bewitch
		_____
contra-	against, opposite	contradict/contraception
		_____
counter	opposition	counter-productive/counteract
		_____

Variation

1 Ask students, in pairs, to match up the words with possible prefixes, using Worksheet 3.4b.

2 Answers are:

antiseptic	_dislike_
a/anaerobic	_enlighten_
abnormal	_inform_
administer	_extraterrestrial_
befriend	_international_
contradiction	_transmission_
counterproductive	_prolong_
destabilize (or deform)	_underestimate_

Worksheet 3.4b

Prefixes	Words
anti-	terrestrial
a-/an-	diction
ab	septic
ad-	normal
be-	lighten
contra-	national
counter-	estimate
de-	form
dis-	stabilize
en-	aerobic
in-	minister
extra-	like
inter-	long
trans-	productive
pro-	mission
under-	friend

Photocopiable © Oxford University Press

Follow-up

1   The prefixes listed in Worksheet 3.4b are among the most common in English. Either in a later class, or as homework, ask students to provide meanings and examples for the more specialized prefixes in Worksheet 3.4c below.

Worksheet 3.4c

Find the meanings of the prefixes below, and give several examples of words using them.

circum-	infra-	ultra-	tele-	phon-	chron-	bene-
poly-	hemi-	mono-	peri-	omni-	ante-	circum-
mega-	hyper-	hypo-	syn-	photo-	arti-	mal-
pan-	path-	para-	epi-	phil-	auto-	hydr-
super-	sub-	intra-	phyto-	ortho-	hetero-	dia-

Photocopiable © Oxford University Press

2 In a further follow-up class, deal in a similar way with suffixes.

3 Distribute Worksheet 3.4d. (See website in 'Useful websites', page 125 for complete lists of suffixes.)

4 You will need to explain that suffixes can serve to change a word into a verb, a noun, an adjective, or an adverb. (See also 3.3 'Word formation'.)

5 In pairs, students use Worksheet 3.4d to decide which suffixes create verbs, nouns, adjectives, and adverbs. For each suffix, they should find at least two example words.

Worksheet 3.4d

Some common suffixes in English

-wise	-ness	-ship	-ward(s)	-ist	-er
___	___	___	___	___	___
-or	-dom	-ful	-ize	-ify	-hood
___	___	___	___	___	___
-istic	-ity	-ility	-ate	-ly	-able
___	___	___	___	___	___
-some	-pathy	-let	-ide	-cracy	-ent
___	___	___	___	___	___
-ster	-ment	-phobia	-ic	-eous	-logy
___	___	___	___	___	___
-philia	-tion	-ial	-worthy	-dict	-less
___	___	___	___	___	___
-ous	-ish	-mania	-al	-ary	-ium
___	___	___	___	___	___

Photocopiable © Oxford University Press

Comments

1 The most important point to note is that a knowledge of and familiarity with prefixes and suffixes is a powerful tool for recognizing and generating more words from those students know already.

2 Like many of the other activities, this is not a one-off learning event. It takes time and many repetitions for this kind of competence to develop.

3 With medium and basic advanced-level groups, start with the Variation, and omit Follow-up step 1.

4 If you are working independently, you can still do all of these activities. Check your answers in your chosen dictionaries.

3.5 Greek and Latin roots

Level Medium and high advanced

Time 60 minutes, plus follow-up

Aims To introduce students to Greek and Latin roots in English words; to show how they can use this information to increase their word store; to recognize new words.

Preparation

1 Make enough copies of Worksheet 3.5 for one per student.

2 Make sure that you yourself are familiar with a good range of these Greek and Latin elements and their core meanings. There are many websites containing this kind of information. A simple Internet search for 'English words with Greek and Latin roots' yields over 195,000 sites! (See 'Useful websites', page 125 for a list containing several hundred such roots.)

Worksheet 3.5

Some Greek or Latin roots

Read examples 1 and 2, then try to find words which use the other roots listed.

1 voc- (vocabulary, vocal, advocate, invoke, invocation, vociferous, revoke)

2 terr- (territorial, terrace, inter (v), territory, terrestrial, terrain)

loc-	pop-	gen-	fluent-	hydr	log-	spect-
————	————	————	————	————	————	————
electr-	elect-	erect-	spir-	sent-/sens-	liter-	num-
————	————	————	————	————	————	————
germ-	graph-	greg-	gyno-	nov-	term-	vert-
————	————	————	————	————	————	————
eco-	anthrop-	arch-	cred-	mit-/miss-	log-	leg-
————	————	————	————	————	————	————
erg-	flect-/flex-	frac-/frag-	grav-	man-	bas-	lect-
————	————	————	————	————	————	————
spec-	merg-	graph-	sec-	seq-	scienc-	
————	————	————	————	————	————	

Photocopiable © Oxford University Press

Procedure

1 Distribute Worksheet 3.5. Then conduct a discussion about roots. Explain that a root is like an old fragment of meaning from another language, usually an ancient one, which has embedded itself in a number of English words. These words continue to carry something of the meaning of the root. Use the examples from the sheet to illustrate this (*voc-*, has the root meaning of *call* and this ancient meaning echoes in all the words derived from it, such as *vocal*, *vocation*. Likewise, *terr-*, which has the meaning of *earth*).

2 Students now work in pairs or threes. Allocate a different row in the worksheet to each pair or group. They should try to come up with as many words with these roots as possible. Allow 15 minutes for this. They may use dictionaries if they wish, though this will not always be a help.

3 Collect examples from groups in a feedback session and note these on the board. Make sure that the words they choose are actual examples of the root. For example *November* contains *nov-* but it is not a root with the meaning *new*, whereas words like *innovation, novel, novice* contain genuine roots with this meaning.

4 Now ask students in pairs to join to make groups of 4–6. The new groups examine the words so far discovered and try to find additional words. They then try to come up with the meaning of the roots in question. For example: *loc-* has something to do with *location* or *place*, *spir-* with *breathing*, *greg-* with *togetherness*, etc. Allow 15 minutes for this, then conduct a class feedback session, noting any interesting cases.

5 Finally, make sure that students understand just how a knowledge of roots can help them to recognize new vocabulary and to extend their own word store.

Follow-up

This is an activity which can be set as homework fairly regularly. Students should keep a careful record of new words that use particular roots in their language notebook. (See also 1.5 'Keeping a language notebook/file'.)

Comments

1 The key point about roots is that they help students to form associative networks of words which share the same ancestors. The ghosts of meaning which lurk beneath the surface of words help to retain vocabulary and to develop a feel for the spirit of the language.

2 If you are working independently, this is an ideal activity for you. You can make use of the abundance of material on the Internet to research new roots and check on their meanings. (See 'Useful websites', page 125.)

3.6 New words

Level All levels

Time 60 minutes, plus follow-up

Aims To raise students' awareness of vocabulary change in English; to show the various mechanisms by which new words are coined.

Preparation

1 Make enough copies of Worksheets 3.6a and 3.6b for one per student. Make sure that you know the meanings of all the words yourself.

2 If possible, have available copies of dictionaries of new words. (See 'Sample text references' page 121.)

Worksheet 3.6a

What do all these words have in common?

fractal	backslash	laptop	shopaholic	sleaze
bioethics	carbon tax	cashback	spin doctor	grunge
hacker	ditzy	biohazardous	spam	rebrand
spreadsheet	flatline (*v*)	alcopop	wind farm	cellphone
readathon	nukemare	carbon tax	cutting edge (*adj*)	pop-up (*n*)
technofreak	clone	glitz	zapper	prequel
HIV	jack	Kalashnikov	Xerox	skype

Photocopiable © Oxford University Press

Procedure

1 Distribute the copies of Worksheet 3.6a. Allow students five minutes to look at the words, and to suggest what they might have in common. Encourage discussion, including guesses at what the words might mean. Finally, tell them that all of these words entered the English language after 1980. In other words, they are all new words.

> ## Worksheet 3.6b
> **How do new words come about?**
> 1 Through borrowing (*bunker, jamboree, barbecue*)
> 2 Through blends (*brunch, glitz, netizen, baggravation*)
> 3 By making new compounds (*scarecrow, laptop, leapfrog, house-husband, couch-potato, earwitness, carjacking*)
> 4 By using prefixes or suffixes (*workaholic, re-purposing, *mouseless*)
> 5 By giving old words new meanings (*crane, mouse, cool, gay, wicked*)
> 6 By forming a new part of speech (*to parent, to obsess, to enthuse; a negative (n from adj); a rave; so last season*)
> 7 From proper names (*hoover, biro, nicotine, spam, bikini, kleenex, tampax*)
> 8 By clipping (*mike* from *microphone*, *sync* from *synchronize*, *exam* from *examination*)
> 9 By occupying vacant spaces in the sound system (*spum, *plute, flegg*)
> 10 By occupying vacant spaces in the morphological system (* milkified, *wowify)
> 11 By using acronyms (AIDS, DVD, SEAMEO, FAQ, BBC)
> *indicates a word which does not yet exist!

Photocopiable © Oxford University Press

2 Remind students that every language is always changing, with new words coming in and going out all the time. This is especially true of English because of its role as an international language. Ask for suggestions about how new words are formed. Allow about ten minutes for this.

3 Distribute Worksheet 3.6b and work through it with the class, finding additional examples where possible.

4 Students then work in pairs and match words from Worksheet 3.6a with processes from Worksheet 3.6b. Can they find examples of all eleven processes?

Variation 1

Words in waiting 1

Explain that English phonology permits certain combinations of sounds in CVC (Consonant–Vowel–Consonant) combinations. Some of these are realized as actual words. For example, with the ending *-ate*, we can find: *hate, late, gate, mate*, but we do not find: *shate, shrate, yate*. Let students discover for themselves which words have and have not been realized for the following CVC combinations: *-ite, -end, -ind, -eem, -ond, -eel.*

Variation 2

Words in waiting 2

Many new words are waiting to become real when formed from prefixes. Let them decide what the following, as yet unrealized, words might mean: *cybertrough, *cyberslut, *cyberglut. Then experiment with inventing new words with the prefixes: *hyper-, under-, over-, psycho-, mega-.*

Comments

1 Becoming aware of just how quickly the vocabulary of English is changing and of the systematic processes of change is a really important part of becoming an advanced learner. The information here is also linked to Activities 3.3, 3.4, and 3.5.

2 If you are working independently, you can do all of these activities, though it is best if you have at least one other student or a teacher to work with.

3.7 Loanwords

Level All levels

Time 60 minutes, plus follow-up

Aims To raise awareness of the large number of English words borrowed from other languages; to show how awareness can help extend and deepen vocabulary knowledge.

Preparation

1 Make enough copies of Worksheet 3.7 for one per student. Make sure that you have checked on the origins of these words (*chaos* from Greek, *alcohol* from Arabic, *amok* from Malay, etc.).

2 Check on origins of loanwords in English using one of the many websites. (See 'Useful websites', page 125.)

Procedure

1 Ask students about any English words or phrases which have been borrowed into their own languages. Collect and share examples.

2 Extend the discussion to words borrowed into English from other languages. You can start by eliciting foreign words associated with food: *restaurant, café, pizza, marinade, banana, coffee*, etc. Then extend the discussion to other topic areas, like fashion: *chic, svelte, perfume, mode*.

3 Distribute Worksheet 3.7. Ask if anyone knows or can guess which languages these words came from. If you have a multinational group, you should get quite a few correct answers.

4 Students work in pairs. They use their dictionaries to find the origin of as many of the words on the worksheet as possible. Allow 15 minutes for this. Then students report back with their findings.

Worksheet 3.7

Words borrowed from other languages

chaos	cereal	thug	banana	alcohol
_____	_____	_____	_____	_____
soliloquy	delta	persecute	perfume	volatile
_____	_____	_____	_____	_____
yam	tariff	cotton	nicotine	loot
_____	_____	_____	_____	_____
hinterland	sputnik	malaria	elastic	tsunami
_____	_____	_____	_____	_____
envelope	pyjama	mosquito	anecdote	amok
_____	_____	_____	_____	_____

Follow-up

1 Encourage students to open a loanwords section in their vocabulary notebooks, and to update it regularly.

2 Encourage them to get into the habit of consulting an etymological dictionary as part of their ongoing acquisition of new words. *The Oxford Dictionary of Word Histories* is a good place to start.

Comments

1 The history of words is part of their flavour and can give us powerful clues to their meanings. It is worth pointing out that loanwords have been an important part of the overall development of the English language. Make the distinction however between words borrowed hundreds of years ago, like *beef*, and more recent borrowings, like *tsunami*. The older borrowings will usually have changed both their pronunciation and their meanings, whereas the more recent ones are relatively unchanged.

2 Loanwords have become increasingly important in English as the language has developed as an international medium of communication. All languages change and grow. Some words enter the language, others die. The rate of change in English is faster than in most other languages, however, so advanced users of the language need to try to keep up with the changes.

3.8 Double trouble

Level All levels (but see Comments below)

Time 60 minutes, plus follow-up

Aims To raise students' awareness of common doublets in English.

Preparation

Make enough copies of Worksheet 3.8 for one per student. Also make sure that there are plenty of copies of reliable learner's dictionaries available.

Worksheet 3.8

Work with a partner and two learners' dictionaries. How many of these double phrases can you find in your dictionaries?

weak and feeble	down and out	meek and mild
born and bred	house and home	thick and thin
wheeling and dealing	movers and shakers	fine and dandy
the great and the good	spick and span	straight and narrow
short and sweet	give and take	open and shut
hard and fast	over and above	profit and loss
fast and loose	tooth and claw	hand and foot
lean and hungry	ins and outs	fair and square
hit and run	dead and buried	well and good

Photocopiable © Oxford University Press

Procedure

1 Introduce the topic of double phrases in English by eliciting examples drawn from everyday life: *bed and breakfast, salt and pepper, fish and chips, mustard and cress.* You might mention that many pub signs in England also take this form: *The Dog and Duck, The Fox and Hounds, The Crown and Anchor, The George and Dragon, The Horse and Groom,* etc. There seems to be a great attraction in English towards this kind of double structure. Here are a few more quirky or unusual ones: *The Moon and Mushroom, The Eagle and Child, The Lamb and Flag, The Bull and Bush, The Boot and Slipper.* Students may like to speculate about the origin of these names!

2 Distribute Worksheet 3.8. Students work in pairs to check these phrases in their dictionaries. Allow 15 minutes for this. Then discuss how many of them are not listed. Can they think of any more such phrases they have met in their reading or have heard? (Some possible examples: *on and off, round and about, through and through, ups and downs, life and limb, life and death, black and white, home and dry, checks and balances, bits and bobs, spits and spats, sick and tired, slap and tickle, feast or famine, hammer and tongs, skin and bone, name and shame, pins and needles, plain and simple.*)

3 Again in pairs, students try to find words which commonly collocate with these doublets. For example, … *born and bred in London, profit and loss account, a lean and hungry look,* … *I need to see it in black and white.*

4 If there is time, discuss the literary devices these phrases often exploit. These include rhyming (*wheeling and dealing, hard and fast*); alliteration (*bright and breezy*); or repetition of the same meaning (*over and above*); opposites (*give and take*).

Variation

For basic advanced-level groups, concentrate on the more common everyday doublets, like *fish and chips, knife and fork, heaven and earth.* How many can they find?

Follow-up

1 Students conduct a homework project. Allow two weeks for them to collect as many more examples of doublets as they can. These can be derived from dictionary searches, Internet searches, or wide-ranging reading. They compile a complete list to bring to class.

2 Extend the project to look for examples of two-word combinations such as:

chitchat, ping-pong, tip-top, sing-song, knick-knack, shilly-shally, zigzag, see-saw, tick tock, willy-nilly, fiddle-faddle, mishmash, bigwig, ding-dong, teeny-weeny, powwow, namby-pamby, mumbo-jumbo, argy-bargy, tittle-tattle, goody-goody, hoity-toity, flip-flop, hanky-panky, hocus-pocus, hobnob.

3 Again note and discuss how often two-word combinations exploit rhyme and alliteration.

Comments

The main point of these activities is to raise students' awareness of this phenomenon so that they will be on the lookout when reading or listening to English. It is not intended that they should learn long lists of such items.

3.9 Fixed phrases

Level   All levels

Time   60 minutes, plus follow-up

Aims   To draw students' attention to the frequent use of 'prefabs' in English; to encourage use of prefabs appropriately in their use of English.

Preparation

1   Collect a range of examples of 'prefabs' or 'polywords'. These are usually short phrases which are not constructed word by word but which are learnt and used as single chunks. (See Worksheet 3.9 for a small sample.) Make enough copies of the worksheet for one per student.

Worksheet 3.9

Polywords or prefabs

you know	in fact	as a matter of fact	at any rate
for that matter	all in all	by and large	once and for all
by the way	if you like	so to speak	for example
time and again	no doubt about it	in my view	from time to time
as we all know	in point of fact	by the time	in part
more or less	over the top	at the end of the day	at this moment in time

---

2   Find a text which contains a number of examples of polywords. Here is a sample text but you should try to find your own. Make enough copies for one per student.

Sample text

> I keep trying to remember when it all started, and how it all started. There wasn't one particular thing I remember but just a lot of small things. Kids pick up a lot of vibes from the atmosphere and from what goes on around them. Sometimes it's just a vague feeling of unease, a feeling that something is not quite right, that things have changed in a way you can't describe but it is a feeling that is real. And that's how it was for me, I think. It was like a virus—something sick in the air, invisible but definitely there. It's only now, when I think back on everything, that I can see the pattern. At the time, it was no more than a vague feeling in the pit of my stomach, a feeling of threat, of insecurity that gradually replaced the feelings of innocent happiness.

Alan Maley, *The Best of Times?*

Procedure

1 Introduce the idea of polywords to the class. Essentially, these are more or less fixed phrases which are stored as wholes in memory. Give just one or two examples, such as *more or less*, or *such as*. Then elicit more from the class.

2 Distribute Worksheet 3.9. Students work in pairs to create sentences using these items. Allow 15 minutes for this. Then check the sentences.

3 Allow another 10 minutes for them to come up with other polywords in English. Check these together.

4 Distribute the text you have chosen (see the sample text above). Ask them to underline any phrases they think are polywords.

Follow-up

1 For the next class, ask each student to bring in a text from a newspaper, a magazine, or a novel, in which they have underlined polywords. They will work in threes, exchanging their texts and discussing the polywords they have identified.

2 In a later class, encourage students to separate such polywords into two classes: those that cannot be changed at all, and those which are more open-ended. For example, *as a matter of fact* is not normally changeable. We cannot say, *as a matter of fiction* or *as an item of fact*. But *how it was for me* could be changed into *how it was for you, … for them, … for us*. And some fixed phrases leave even more space for substitution. For example, *the (-er), the (-er)* can become *The bigger the better* or *The more I see her, the less I like her*, etc. Thus these polywords are no more than fixed frameworks with potential gaps to be filled.

4

Focus on grammar

At this level, there is not much point in going back over the kind of sentence grammar which students have encountered repeatedly in the course of their language learning. Instead, the focus will be on the grammar of words, the grammar of texts, the differences between spoken and written grammar, and how grammar and meaning are related overall.

4.1 Chunking a text

Level All levels

Time 60 minutes, plus follow-up

Aims To draw students' attention to the relationship between grammar and meaning in a text; to link speech with writing through oral reading of a text.

Preparation

Choose a text 10–15 lines long. This can be on any subject, factual or fictional. Print enough copies for one per student.

Sample text

> The narrow road to the top of Nandi Hills winds up in a series of over thirty tight hairpin bends to a point over 1500 metres above sea-level. The hills are covered by thorn bushes and eucalyptus trees but there is a lot of bare granite rock exposed to the burning dry heat.

Alan Maley, *He Knows Too Much*

Procedure

1 Distribute your sample text. Students read it silently. Then ask them if they have any questions about it.

2 Tell students that they should prepare to read the text aloud in the clearest way possible. To help themselves do this, they should make pencil marks in the text where they would pause briefly. Allow ten minutes for this.

3 Students now compare their texts in pairs. Give them a few more minutes, then conduct a class discussion. Did students all mark their texts identically? If not, were the differences acceptable or not? Ask students to read aloud any disputed markings. Do they sound right?

4 Discuss their reasons for marking in the places they did. Do the markings correspond with grammatical borderlines between words, phrases, clauses, sentences?

5 If time allows, ask a few students to read the text aloud in the way they have marked it. If not, set preparation for reading it as a homework assignment.

Variation

You can also prepare a text you have marked for pauses, in which some of your markings are wrong. Students discuss in pairs any changes they would make.

Comments

1 Students should get into the habit of marking any text they will have to read publicly. (See also activities in Chapter 8 'Focus on speaking'.)

2 Note that there is no one correct way to chunk a text. Differences may arise from the wish to emphasize certain sections of the text as part of a special interpretation.

3 If you are working independently, you can still do the activity. Try to find a sympathetic person to listen to your reading.

4.2 Spoken grammar

Level All levels

Time 60 minutes, plus regular follow-up

Aims To raise students' awareness of the systematic grammatical properties of informal spoken English; to offer guidelines for accessing further information on this.

Preparation

1 Make sure that you are aware of the systematic features of informal spoken English. Ronald Carter and Michael McCarthy's *The Cambridge Grammar of English* provides more examples.

2 Print out enough copies of Worksheet 4.2 for one per student.

Procedure

1 Lead a discussion about the differences between spoken and written English. List them on the board.

Example

Written	Spoken
carefully planned	*improvised*
formal	*informal*
grammatically correct	*lots of 'mistakes'*
economical	*lots of repetition*
no backtracking/interruptions	*lots of backtracking/interruptions*

Does this mean that spoken English is 'ungrammatical'? Explain that in recent years linguists have been discovering that spoken

Worksheet 4.2
Spoken grammar

Headers
1 That red sports car, the one parked on the corner, is that yours?
2 My ex-girlfriend, Tracy, her Mum just had another baby!
3 The guy with the red beard, he looks weird.
4 That time when you fell through the floor, that was some party!
5 That new housing development over by Kirby, have they finished it yet?
6 The tall one with the shades, I really fancy him.
7 Fiddling the books, he does it all the time.

Tails
1 You'd never believe how daft he is, our Kevin.
2 They're not so bad really, our kids.
3 I never thought about it really, the damage it was doing.
4 He didn't even think about you know, how much it was costing us.
5 They're from South America mainly, this intake.
6 He's not worth bothering about, isn't Dave.
7 It's got a lovely coat, that dog has.
8 I can't stand the smell of it, garlic.

Echoes
1 I'm off to Brazil tomorrow.
   To where?
   Brazil.

2 It looks like a Braque.
   Like a what?
   A Braque. Don't you know who Braque is? Artist, inee?

3 He's got some lovely fresh pollock.
   Fresh what?
   Pollock … it's a fish.

4 I thought it was unfortunate, the way he spoke to her.
   Unfortunate, why?
   Not very tactful. You know …

Vague language
1 He's more like a sort of, you know, middleman, know what I mean?
2 We had plenty of snacks and stuff.
3 There was something like 50 protesters there and that.
4 I haven't got much time for that type of thing, if you see what I mean.
5 It was all a bit of a mess, messy like, if you get me.
6 It all went sort of pear-shaped really, a bit of a … you know … .

English has its own systematic grammar. In this class, students will be looking at just four of these typical features of spoken English grammar, though there are many, many more.

2 Distribute copies of Worksheet 4.2. Allow students about ten minutes to look at them in pairs. Then collect comments.

3 Divide the class into four groups. Allocate one of the features to each group: headers, tails, echoes, and vague language. Over the coming two weeks, ask each group to collect examples of their feature from broadcasts, television programmes, or real conversations. They should keep a careful record of what was said, by whom, and where/when. Then hold a follow-up class in which they discuss their findings.

Comments

1 See also Douglas Biber, Susan Conrad, and Geoffrey Leech, *A Student Grammar of Spoken and Written English*, for more information on spoken grammar.

2 If you are working independently, you can still carry out the activity, choosing one or more features to look out for.

4.3 Rules from examples: word grammar

Level All levels

Time 60 minutes, repeated regularly

Aims To use authentic data in the form of concordance lines for students to work out grammatical rules.

Preparation

You need to print out concordance lines for the following words: *talk, say, speak.*

Sample text

> **talk**
> ... the message and we'll **talk** to you, but we ...
> ... the two boys to **talk** about the others on ...
> ... I could come and **talk** to him about the...
> ... a good deal of **talk** about that, but I ...
> ... When Tweedledum and Tweedledee **talk** to Alice they are almost talking ...
> ... me the full story. **talk** about leading me ...

> **say**
> ... I know, but I dare **say** it's simply a case ...
> ... As you breathe in, **say** to yourself 'relaxation is' ...
> ... I heard my brother **say** to Dad how sorry he ...
> ... there is normally between **say** a employer and an ...
> ... Right, but let's **say** that you're not prepared ...
> ... how come then people **say**, What part of Lancashire ...

> **speak**
> ... All of these books **speak** of a someone other ...
> ... assessment even when they **speak** fluent English. This is ...
> ... said, 'I must just **speak** to John; he's over ...
> ... consider having the mayor **speak** at a breakfast at ...
> ... possible for him to **speak** with the manager about ...
> ... we often think and **speak** of decisions and the ...

Procedure

1 Discuss with students the criteria for drawing up rules. For example, a grammatical rule should be accurate, comprehensive, clearly stated/unambiguous, worth stating, and helpful to learners.

2 Tell students that they are going to formulate rules for three common English words. To help them formulate the rules they will have access to concordance lines. Allow 30 minutes for this, working in pairs or individually if they prefer.

3 Check on progress. How many rules have they drawn up? Note them on the board and discuss how well they conform to the criteria for a good rule in step 1 above.

4 Ask students to complete the activity for homework. Over the following weeks, set other groups of words. For example, *listen, hear, catch, get* (in the sense of *hear/understand*).

Comments

If you are working independently, you can still do the activity, provided you have access to an online concordance. (See 'Useful websites', page 125.)

4.4 Ambiguity

Level All levels

Time 60 minutes

Aims To activate students' grammatical knowledge to 'disambiguate' sentences with more than one meaning; to sharpen students' awareness of the need for clarity in writing.

Preparation

Print out a worksheet list of ambiguous sentences, enough for one per student. Worksheet 4.4 is an example, but you can find more on various websites. (See 'Useful websites', page 125.)

Procedure

1 Check that everyone understands what ambiguity means: something that is not clear because it has more than one possible meaning. Write up one of the sentences from Worksheet 4.4 and discuss how it is ambiguous. For example *They hit the man with a bag*. This could mean *The man they hit was carrying a bag* or *They used a bag to hit the man*.

2 Distribute the worksheets. Students can work alone, in pairs, or in groups of three. They should try to disambiguate as many of the sentences as possible in 15 minutes. They can do this either by writing out two sentences in which the meanings are clear (as in the example in step 1), or by adding information to the sentence, for example … *remove all your clothes from the machine…*, or by explanation.

3 After 15 minutes, go through the sentences, asking for students' disambiguations. Ask: *What have you learnt from this activity?*

Worksheet 4.4
Ambiguous sentences

1 I said I would see you on Tuesday.
2 I found a smouldering cigarette left by a horse.
3 We don't just serve hamburgers, we serve people.
4 The train left the station crowded and dirty.
5 The visitor saw the astronomer with the telescope.
6 Why go elsewhere to be cheated when you can come here?
7 Woman without her man is a savage.
8 You will be very fortunate to get this man to work for you.
9 I am pleased to say that this man is a former colleague of mine.
10 I once shot an elephant in my pyjamas.
11 This is the worst disaster in California since I was elected. (Governor Pat Brown)
12 Students hate annoying professors.
13 They hit the man with a bag.
14 Please remove all your clothes when the light goes out. (in a Laundromat)
15 Drop your trousers here for best results. (in a tailor's shop)
16 We dispense with accuracy. (in a chemist's shop)
17 Best place to take a leak. (at a garage radiator repair shop)

Comments

1 In order to be able to disambiguate the sentences, it is first necessary to 'see' what the two meanings are. This already requires quite a complex piece of mental processing. In order to clarify the meanings, they must also be able to generate new sentences, which again involves calling upon all their grammatical resources. The activity then becomes quite a powerful grammatical exercise tool.

2 Ambiguity is also the basis for puns, where it is used on purpose. Some students may like to collect puns in English, many of which crop up in newspaper headlines and shop signs. For example, 'A fez of the heart' (in a travel magazine) can be read as 'Affairs of the heart'. Remember, however, that humour in a foreign language is always a tricky area!

4.5 How many ways?

Level   All levels

Time   15–30 minutes, repeated regularly

Aims   To give students practice in 'grammaticizing lexis'; to activate their full repertory of grammatical structures.

Preparation

Prepare a set of content word strings which could be combined into many different sentences. Here are some examples:

- accident, dog, run, road, woman
- computer, break, scientist, repair
- come, time, stop, bomb, quickly
- trouble, cause, actor, elephant, feed
- money, waste, lose, investments, luck

Procedure

1   Have a brief discussion with students about the different ways the same content words might be combined grammatically, for example, the string *drink, health, teenagers, know, problem*. This could generate the following sentences:

   - We know that teenagers who drink may have a problem with their health.
   - It is well known that drink is a problem for teenagers' health.
   - Teenagers who drink do not know that they may have a health problem.
   - What we know about teenage drinking is that it is a problem for their health.
   - How can we be sure that what we know about teenage drinking is connected with health problems?

2   Write just one of the above strings on the board. Students then work in pairs for just ten minutes to write out as many different sentences as they can, based on the words in the string.

3   Collect the examples from each pair. The winning pair is the one with the greatest number of sentences which make sense.

Variation

Instead of giving students a word string, write up a sentence and invite them to reformulate it in as many different ways as possible without changing the meaning. For example:
John married Mary, not Susan.
This could yield many possible sentences:

- It was Mary John married, not Susan.
- Susan wasn't the woman John married, it was Mary.
- What John did was to marry Mary, not Susan.

Comments

This is a relatively light-hearted and brief activity, which can be used as a warm-up activity or as a filler. However, it is a powerful way of rehearsing the many different ways in which words can be grammaticized. One of the major functions of grammar is to tell us how words are connected to form a network of meaning. This activity helps to demonstrate it very clearly.

4.6 My grammar problem

Level All levels

Time 60 minutes, repeated (optional)

Aims To elicit the grammatical problems which worry students most; to encourage them to share practical tips for dealing with such problems.

Preparation

Make sure that you have a generous collection of grammar reference materials available for students to consult.

Procedure

1 Conduct a discussion with students about their English language learning histories. What were the major problems they encountered? Narrow the focus down to grammar. What specific problems did they have with the grammar of English? Then move to the key question: *What is the main grammatical problem you have with English even now?*

2 Ask students to work in groups of four. They exchange with each other the main English grammar problems they feel they still have. Allow 20 minutes for this.

3 Conduct a feedback session in which they report on their findings. Note the problem areas on the board. Then have students vote on the five problems they think are the most important.

4 Allocate one problem to each group. If there are more than five groups, the same problem can be given to more than one group. For the rest of the lesson, groups work on gathering as much information as they can to make their problem more understandable. This may involve researching explanations in the reference materials, collecting revealing examples, developing mnemonics for recalling key information, etc.

5 Groups work out of class to complete their work. Set a date for mini-presentations on each of the five problems.

Comments

1 It is not possible to predict accurately what they will list as their problems, as these are specific to each individual. However, it is likely that at least some of the following will be raised: prepositions, phrasal verbs, the treatment of time and use of tenses, modality,

order of adjectives before a noun. You may need to monitor the problems they raise to eliminate trivial issues, such as, the difference between *different from/different to*.

2 Besides hard copy reference materials, students should make use of Internet resources. There are a few possibilities, but note that many websites are not really at an advanced level. They are not always accurate either! (See 'Useful websites', page 125 for grammar websites.)

3 If you are working independently, you can still do the activity by simply listing your three major problems, and using reference materials to elucidate them.

4.7 Simplifying a text

Level High advanced

Time 60 minutes, plus homework

Aims To draw on the full range of students' grammatical knowledge to simplify a complex text; to practise reformulating sentences and texts.

Preparation

1 Find one or more reasonably short texts that are complex in both language and ideas.

Sample text

> Now in all of us, however constituted, but to a degree the greater in proportion as we are intense and sensitive and subject to diversified temptations, and to the greatest possible degree if we are decidedly psychopathic, does the normal evolution of character chiefly consist in the straightening out and unifying of the inner self. The higher and the lower feelings, the useful and the erring impulses, begin by being a comparative chaos within us—they must end by forming a stable system of functions in right subordination. Unhappiness is apt to characterize the period of order-making and struggle. If the individual be of tender conscience and religiously quickened, the unhappiness will take the form of moral remorse and compunction, of feeling inwardly vile and wrong, and of standing in false relations to the author of one's being and appointer of one's spiritual fate. This is the religious melancholy and 'conviction of sin' that have played so large a part in the history of Protestant Christianity.

William James, *The Varieties of Religious Experience*

2 Make enough copies of your chosen text for one per two students.

Procedure

1 Elicit from the students reasons why some texts are so difficult to read. They will probably suggest things like: long, complex sentences, difficult or unusual vocabulary, or unfamiliar subject matter.

2 Explain that they will be working in pairs with just such a text. Their objective will be to make it comprehensible to an average general reader. They could imagine the text as it might appear in 'serious' Sunday newspapers in the UK, which have intelligent but non-specialist readerships.

3 Distribute the text, one per pair. Give them a few minutes to skim-read it. Then ask some leading questions:

- *What is it about?*
- *What seem to be the most difficult and obscure parts of it?*
- *How could it be simplified?*

Agree that it could be simplified by breaking the long, complex sentences into shorter ones, by simplifying some of the longer descriptive phrases, by summarizing parts of it, by changing the order of information in sentences, and by using simpler vocabulary.

4 Then let students work in pairs on the text for about 15 minutes. In a feedback session, collect examples of the ways different pairs have gone about simplification, and discuss and evaluate them with the class.

5 They will almost certainly not have finished by the end of the class, so ask them to complete the task as homework, and plan a future class for further discussion of the completed versions.

Comments

1 Reducing a complex and difficult text to a simpler version demands a highly sophisticated control of grammar, vocabulary, and textual organization. It is therefore both very demanding and very useful for truly advanced students.

2 You may wish to repeat the activity on a later occasion, asking students to contribute texts from their own fields of specialization.

3 If you are working independently, you can follow the suggestions in Procedure above, but you will not be able to compare with a fellow student, unless you have an online 'study-buddy'. You may also find it useful to compare an original with a simplified text (see Activity 5.6) and note the way in which the original has been simplified.

4.8 Correcting

Level All levels

Time 60 minutes

Aims To activate students' accumulated grammatical knowledge to correct a faulty text.

Preparation

1 Find at least three different texts which contain a large number of grammatical errors. You may wish to use written work from lower-level classes, with names removed of course!

Sample text

Respected Sir,

I Kindly Inform you that my residential is near to your House. I please to Inform that your Night Watchman Commiting Lot of trouble to the Neibours and other public and Servents in your house and sorounding. Mostly He is Eve-teasing servent maidens. Last Wednesday he fought with the care driver of your IIIrd Bunglow unnessearly along with the duty police man posted in your Bunglow. Some time before same like this they have told to the Night Area watchman not to come by the side with out their permission. Actually we don't know why he said like that to watchman. please you should concentrate about this. My wish Better you sack him out from Bunglow. Even the posted policeman Involved in this casses along with him, because both used to drink particularly in the night time. This matter was warned by the lady who is in charge of your house. But they donot bother about and still they are in same head condition. please take action kindly with out problem goes heavy.

I hope, you will take action about the Information as I please. I will be very greetful about it.

Thanking you.

Yours sincerely. (letter not signed)

2 Make enough copies of your three chosen texts for each third of the class to have a different one per pair.

Procedure

1 Explain that you will be giving out some texts with large numbers of errors of all kinds—spelling, punctuation, word choice, grammar. The task is for students to correct as many of the errors as possible.

2 Distribute the texts to pairs of students. Each text should be worked on by an equal number of pairs. Allow 15 minutes for corrections. These should be noted neatly on the text itself.

3 Pairs then exchange texts with other pairs working on different scripts. They then work in groups of four to discuss the corrections made. Allow about 15 minutes for this.

4 Conduct a feedback session where errors are discussed by the whole class.

Comments

1 Students enjoy correcting other people's mistakes. But in addition, the activity is useful in developing a critical eye for grammatical and other errors.

2 If you are working independently, you can still do the activity. It will be better, though, if you have an email friend who can exchange texts with you, so that you can comment on each other's work.

4.9 Teaching a grammar point

Level All (but see below)

Time 60 minutes' preparation, plus homework, plus two further class hours for presentations

Aims To activate students' research and presentation skills; to extend their detailed grammatical knowledge of a particular grammar point.

Preparation

1 Make sure that you have a good selection of grammar reference books available.

2 Prepare a short list of grammatical points which often cause students problems. Include examples at different levels of complexity to cater for weaker students.

Example • When to use *would* and when to use *will*.
 • When to use a passive rather than an active form.
 • Reasons for using nominalization (e.g. The police deported them/ Police deportation took place.).
 • Verbs which do not normally occur with the present progressive, such as *know*, *like*, etc.
 • The differences between the various ways of expressing future time.
 • The present simple tense used for stories, commentaries, and instructions.
 • Avoidance of grammatical repetition. (e.g. *That girl, she ...*)

See also Michael Swan, *Practical English Usage*, for more examples of such difficulties.

Procedure

1 Explain to students that they are going to do some team teaching in groups of three. Either assign one grammar problem per group or distribute the list above and allow students to choose a point from it. Tell them they will have 30 minutes to discuss and research their point and to start preparing a plan for teaching it. Put out the reference books so that they can consult them freely. Make yourself available for advice if needed.

2 After they have done some preparation, hold a class discussion. Suggest that, in preparing their teaching point, they will need to consider the target students' level, the objective, the time available, the materials and examples they will use, and the steps they will go through in their lesson. Write these points on the board and elicit other suggestions from them.

3 Set a presentation date for about two weeks later. Explain that they will need to prepare their lessons in their own time.

4 On the due date, each group of three presents its lesson, using the rest of the class as its 'class', followed by discussion and suggestions for improvement. Depending on the size of the class, this may last one or two class hours.

Variation

With high advanced groups, you can allow them to choose the points for themselves if they prefer.

Comments

1 Being asked to teach something is one of the best ways of really understanding it. In order to teach it, the students have to become thoroughly conversant with all aspects of the problem. This kind of work is usually very motivating, as they become totally absorbed in researching their lesson.

2 See also 4.7 'Simplifying a text', which can be done as a preparation for this activity in identifying possible points for teaching.

5

Focus on reading

All the research evidence available shows that the single most effective way of acquiring, consolidating, and extending language is through extensive reading. Extensive reading involves reading large quantities of text quickly. Texts have to be within the range of ability of the reader and be chosen by the reader. The activities in this chapter are partly designed to foster extensive reading. However, there are some activities which focus on more careful, closer reading, The texts we will encounter at advanced level will not always yield up their meanings to a rapid reading. Moreover, reading speed will vary according to reading purpose. Sometimes we need to read analytically for information, sometimes more rapidly for sheer enjoyment. The main message of the chapter is, however, a simple one—the more you read, the faster you will progress.

5.1 Your reading log

Level All levels

Time 30 minutes to introduce the idea, with regular follow-up

Aims To encourage students to keep a careful record of what they read; to develop a reflective approach to reading.

Preparation

Prepare a sample page of a reading log and make enough copies for one per student.

Procedure

1 Have a brief discussion about the importance of reading in becoming an even more advanced user of English. Explain that the more we read, the better we become at it, and it has spin-off value for writing, and even speaking. So it is worth taking it seriously. Keeping a record of what we read is valuable because it forces us to pay more attention to what we read, it helps us recall what we have read, it is motivating when we look back on what we have read, and it can be helpful for others to hear our opinions about things they might like to read.

2 Discuss books or articles students have read recently. How would they choose to keep a record of them for future reference?

3 Distribute Worksheet 5.1. Explain that you will expect each student to keep their own reading log from now on, and that you will check the logs regularly. Ask students to buy a large format notebook and to rule it off as in the worksheet. If they have a better idea of how to organize it, based on the discussion in step 2 above, fine. Ask them to bring the log to the next class with one or two entries completed.

Comments

1 This activity should be linked with Activity 5.8, 'Book reviews and reports'.

2 If you are working independently, the reading log can be even more important as a motivational and thinking tool. It will help you to read more critically and to reflect more deeply on what you have read.

Worksheet 5.1
My reading log

Monday 2 June

Text type	Short story
Title	*Leaf Like*
Author	Sari Smith
Publisher	?
Length	6 pp.
Time taken	10 minutes
Comments	Complex story about a young woman and her relationship with an older man. A bit confusing in places. Time shifts too complex. Left me feeling confused. A bit too pretentious.
Recommend	Not really

Photocopiable © Oxford University Press

5.2 Increase your reading speed

Level   All levels

Time   15 minutes, plus private reading

Aims   To show students how reading speed can be increased; to emphasize the importance of reading speed without loss of comprehension.

Preparation

In the class before you plan this activity, ask students to bring along one book in English they are reading or plan to read.

Procedure

1 Check that everyone has brought along their book. Explain that increasing reading speed is a key part of becoming an advanced reader. Tell them that the activity you will now show them is something they can do regularly on their own to raise their speed.

2 Ask them to take out their books. At your signal, they start reading. Then stop them after just two minutes. They should mark in pencil where they had got to on the page.

3 They close their books, and you discuss the fact that research shows that increasing reading speed actually increases rather than decreases comprehension. After a few minutes, ask them to open their books again. They should go back to their starting point. On your signal, they again read for exactly two minutes. When they stop, they mark in pencil the point they reached this time.

4 Repeat the procedure a third time. When they finish reading, what do they notice? Everyone will have read further on each occasion of reading. Remind them to do this activity regularly as a kind of toning-up exercise.

Variation

Students read a complete text (about 1000–2000 words) as fast as possible. They record the time taken, and calculate their reading speed in words per minute (wpm). Over a period of time, say a week, they read a number of texts of about the same length in the same way, recording their speed in wpm each time. They will almost certainly notice an increase in speed.

Acknowledgements

I owe the idea for this activity to Bamford and Day, *Extensive Reading Activities for Teaching Language*. I am also indebted to Paul Nation. For his downloadable speed-reading course, see 'Useful websites', page 126.

5.3 Anticipation and prediction

Level All levels

Time 60 minutes, repeated occasionally

Aims To develop faster and more accurate reading through becoming proficient at predicting the words and patterns of a text.

Preparation

Find a text which has a fairly predictable information structure, and possibly quite a lot of repetition. Remove about 50 per cent of the most predictable words in the text. Make enough copies of the text you choose for one per student.

Sample text

Imagine _____ piece _____ land twenty miles long and _____ _____ _____. Picture _____ wild, _____ by animals _____ and large. Now _____ a compact group of sixty human _____ camping _____ _____ middle of this _____. Try _____ _____ yourself sitting _____, as _____ _____ of this tiny _____, with the _____, your landscape, spreading _____ around you farther _____ you _____ _____. No one apart _____ _____ tribe uses _____ vast _____. _____ is _____ exclusive home-range, _____ tribal hunting _____. _____ so often _____ men in your _____ set _____ in _____ of _____. The _____ gather fruit and _____. The _____ play _____ around _____ camp _____, imitating _____ hunting _____ of _____ _____. If _____ _____ is successful _____ _____ in size, a splinter _____ will _____ _____ _____ colonize a new _____. _____ by little _____ species will _____. _____ a piece _____ _____ twenty _____ _____ _____ twenty _____ wide. _____ it _____, inhabited _____ machines and _____. _____ visualize a _____ group _____ six million _____ _____ _____ _____ _____ middle _____ _____ _____. See _____ _____ there, with _____ complexity _____ _____ huge city _____ out all _____ _____, _____ than _____ _____ _____. Now _____ these two _____.

Desmond Morris, *The Human Zoo*

Procedure

1 Conduct a brief discussion on the importance of being able to predict what words will occur next when we are reading. For example, good readers can usually predict the word or phrase on the next page before they actually turn the page. Mention that it is not just words that we predict: texts have a predictable shape too, and that facilitates prediction and comprehension.

2 Hand out the gapped text you have chosen. Allow 15 minutes for students to complete it. The complete text of the sample text appears on page 77.

3 Conduct class feedback, with discussion of alternatives for the slots. If the students did not complete the text, elicit words for the remaining gaps. Then discuss how it was possible to complete the text. For example, point out how the second paragraph mirrors the shape of the first paragraph.

Comments

1 From time to time, when you find a good example, draw attention to the way the structure of texts is also predictable. (See also 5.5, 'Narrow reading'.)

2 This is an activity your students can do on their own from time to time, using a bank of gapped texts you build up for them.

3 If you are working independently, you could ask a friend to choose a suitable text, duplicate it, and white out every third word on the copy. When you receive it, try to complete the gapped text and then compare it with the original.

5.4 The reading circle

Level All levels

Time 30 minutes to set up, plus regular discussion sessions

Aims To create a community of committed readers; to encourage students to read longer texts.

Preparation

Decide on a selection of possible titles for your students to read, based on their interests and proficiency levels. The titles may be fiction or non-fiction, and to begin with they may be long newspaper or magazine articles. Prepare a display of these titles or articles. You will need to ensure that there are sufficient copies of all titles for one per student.

Procedure

1 Introduce students to the idea of 'reading circles'. Essentially, a reading circle is a small group of readers who agree to read the same title within a certain time. Two weeks is a reasonable time-frame for most titles. One or more students prepare a report or discussion paper. The group then meets on the appointed date and discusses what everyone has read. (You may wish to have available copies of *The Oxford Bookworms Club Reading Circles: Teacher's Guide*, editor Mark Furr, which gives detailed information on setting up a reading circle.)

2 Allow students time to browse through the display of titles or articles. Then hold a vote on the title they would like to read first.

3 Now agree a date for the meeting of the reading circle, preferably out-of-class time and within 2–3 weeks. The group should also appoint two members who will prepare a report and lead the discussion as rapporteurs.

4 On the agreed date the group meets and discusses, as critically as possible, the title they have all read. The discussion will follow the brief presentations by the two rapporteurs.

5 The group then agrees a new title and different rapporteurs, and sets a date for the next meeting.

Comments

1 Readers' circles provide invaluable motivation and support for reading. They also foster a community feeling—a first step in joining the confederacy of readers.

2 For basic-level advanced readers, it may be good to start with Level 6 graded readers from one of the major published series.

3 After students have read two or three books, elicit suggestions from them for titles they would like to read next.

4 If you are working independently, you can still do this activity. You will not have the benefit of input from other students, but you may have other opportunities. You could join or create a reading circle, or share your reading experience with friends or email friends. (See 'Further reading', page 123.)

5.5 Narrow reading

Level All levels

Time 40 minutes, plus follow-up

Aims To facilitate more effective reading by giving students texts which are similar in one way or another.

Preparation

Collect about ten texts on the same topic. One good source is newspapers or magazines dealing with a current issue, such as global food shortages, international sports events, a celebrity with problems, etc. Make sure there are enough copies available for one per student.

Procedure

1 Remind students that when we read, we constantly map the new material we are reading onto what we already know or have read about the topic. If we did not do this, we would have to construct every piece of information afresh each time we met it. So, we can make our reading more efficient by reading within a narrow range, because a lot of the information will be common to all the texts.

2 Make the texts available at the front of the class. Students collect a text each. Set a time limit of 20 minutes. Within that time students must read as many of the texts as possible. As soon as they finish one text, they replace it and take another.

3 Did they find the reading getting easier as they read more texts? Ask them to collect any texts they have not yet read to take home to read.

Variation 1

Narrow reading can be done in other ways, too. You could encourage students to read a number of books or stories by the same author. Most authors have a particular way of writing, and we get accustomed to this as we read more of their work. This facilitates faster reading of their work.

Variation 2

Another alternative is to focus on texts from a specific genre. These may be short text types, such as advertisements, or longer ones, such as short stories. They may also be from genres the students need for their professions: manufacturer's specifications for medicines or drugs, operating instructions for machinery, company reports, etc.

5.6 Comparing originals with simplified texts

Level All levels

Time 60 minutes, plus homework

Aims To enable students to read texts critically; to compare different ways of conveying the same information; to evaluate different versions of the 'same' text.

Preparation

1 You will need to find a novel which has been simplified at several different levels. There are plenty of much-simplified titles in a number of graded readers lists. Select an identical episode from the original and two different simplified versions of the episode.

2 Make enough copies for students to work on the extracts in groups of three. Here are examples from the scene in *Jane Eyre* where she returns to find Mr Rochester blind, after the fire at his house.

Sample text 1 **Original text**

> 'Is that what he rang for?' I asked.
> 'Yes; he always has candles brought in at dark, though he is blind.'
> 'Give the tray to me; I will carry it in.'
> I took it from her hand: she pointed me out the parlour door. The tray shook as I held it; the water spilt from the glass; my heart struck my ribs loud and fast. Mary opened the door for me, and shut it behind me.
> This parlour looked gloomy. A neglected handful of fire burnt low in the grate; and leaning over it, with his head supported against the high, old-fashioned mantelpiece, appeared the blind tenant of the room. His old dog, Pilot, lay on one side, removed out of the way, and coiled up as if afraid of being inadvertently trodden upon. Pilot pricked up his ears when I came in; then he jumped up with a yelp and a whine, and bounded towards me: he almost knocked the tray from my hands. I set it on the table; then patted him, and said softly, 'Lie down!' Mr Rochester turned mechanically to see what the commotion was; but as he saw nothing, he returned and sighed.
> 'Give me the water, Mary,' he said.
> I approached him with the now only half-filled glass; Pilot followed me, still excited.
> 'What is the matter?' he inquired.
> 'Down, Pilot,' I again said. He checked the water on its way to his lips, and seemed to listen: he drank, and put his glass down. 'This is you, Mary, is it not?'
> 'Mary is in the kitchen,' I answered.

Charlotte Brontë, *Jane Eyre*

Sample text 2   Version 1

> The servant filled a glass with water, and placed it on a tray together with candles.
>
> 'Is that what he rang for?' I asked.
>
> 'Yes, he always has candles brought in when it gets dark, though he is blind.'
>
> 'Give me the tray. I will carry it in.'
>
> I took it from her hand. It shook as I held it. The water spilt from the glass, and my heart beat loud and fast. John's wife opened the door, and shut it behind me.
>
> The sitting room did not look cheerful. A small, neglected fire burnt low in the fireplace, and leaning over it was the blind owner of the room. His old dog, Pilot, lay on one side, but jumped up and ran to find me, almost knocking the tray from my hand. I set it on the table, and said softly, 'Lie down!' Mr Rochester turned to see what the disturbance was, but remembering his weakness, moved his head back again.
>
> 'Give me the water,' he said.
>
> I approached him. Pilot followed me, still excited.
>
> Down, Pilot!' I said again. He paused with the water halfway to his lips, and seemed to listen. He drank and put the glass down.
>
> 'Who is this? Who is this?' he demanded. 'Answer me—speak again!'
>
> 'Pilot knows me, and John and his wife. I have just come,' I answered.

Charlotte Brontë, *Jane Eyre*, ed. Evelyn Atwell

Sample text 3   Version 2

> 'But he may not want to see you,' warned Mary, as we sat together in the kitchen. 'He refuses to see anybody except us.' She was lighting some candles. 'He always wants candles in the sitting room when it's dark, even though he's blind.'
>
> 'Give them to me, Mary,' I said. 'I'll take them to him.'
>
> The blind man was sitting near the neglected fire in the dark room.
>
> 'Put down the candles, Mary,' he sighed.
>
> 'Here they are, sir,' I said.
>
> 'That *is* Mary, isn't it?' he asked, listening carefully.
>
> 'Mary's in the kitchen,' I answered.

Charlotte Brontë, *Jane Eyre*, retold by Clare West

Procedure

1   Explain that many 'real' books are simplified to make them readable by lower-level students. This is obviously not the case for advanced students! Tell your class they are going to analyse the ways in which simplification is carried out.

2 Hand out the three texts you chose to each group of three. They should first read the original as quickly as possible. They then compare it with one of the two simplifications and note in detail how the original has been simplified. For example, by omitting actions or objects or dialogue, by using simpler vocabulary or grammar, etc. Allow 20 minutes for this.

3 Conduct class feedback, noting the simplification devices used. Use prompt questions, such as:

- *Which text did you prefer, the original or the simplified version?*
- *Why?*
- *Did you find the task a challenge?*
- *Why would you wish/not wish to read simplified rather than original versions?*

Variation

Distribute a short extract from an original text and ask students to simplify it. They should first decide on their criteria: overall length, vocabulary, sentence length and complexity, simplification by omission of 'redundant' scenes, etc. When they have finished, give them one of the published simplified versions to compare with their own.

Comments

This activity really forces students, as readers, to probe the essence of a text, and to ask some sometimes disturbing questions:

- *What is the quality of an original which makes it unique?*
- *Is it possible that a simplification is actually 'better' than the original?*
- *If simplifications are a quicker way of accessing books, why not just read summaries of the plots?*

These, and other, questions are all worth probing with advanced students because they go to the heart of why texts are valued, and how useful it is to defend a full critical literacy in a contemporary culture which puts value on more, faster, and easier.

5.7 Comparing texts

Level All levels

Time 60 minutes

Aims To develop students' critical reading through comparison of texts.

Preparation

1 Find two texts on a similar theme or with similar contents. There are plenty of examples from literary texts (see page 73). Alternatively, two articles from different newspapers covering the same story would be suitable. Make enough copies of the texts you choose for one per student.

2 Hand out the first text one week before the class. Tell students to read it carefully so that they are thoroughly familiar with it before they come to class.

Sample text 1

> Some say my dad's corrupt and I'm his money launderer. Well, it's true enough. People are robbing the country blind, and if the choice is between being held up at gunpoint or holding the gun, only a madman would choose to hand over his wallet rather than fill it with someone else's cash. Why do you think my father got into it? He was a soldier. He served in '71. He saw what was going on. And he decided he wasn't going to wait around to get shot in the back while people divided up the country. He wanted his piece. And I want mine.
>
> What's the alternative? You have to have money these days. The roads are falling apart, so you need a Pajero or a Land Cruiser. The phone lines are erratic, so you need a mobile. The colleges are overrun with fundos who have no interest in getting an education, so you have to go abroad. And that's ten lakhs a year mind you. Thanks to electricity theft there will always be shortages, so you have to have a generator. The police are corrupt and ineffective, so you need private security guards. It goes on and on. People are pulling their pieces out of the pie, and the pie is getting smaller, so if you love your family, you'd better take your piece now, while there's some left. That's what I'm doing. And if anyone isn't doing it, it's because they're locked out of the kitchen.
>
> Guilt isn't a problem, by the way. Once you've started, there's no way to stop, so there's nothing to be guilty about. Ask yourself this: If you're me, what do you do now? Turn yourself in to the police, so some sadistic, bare-chested Neanderthal can beat you to a pulp while you await trial? Publish a full apology in the newspapers? Take the Karakoram Highway up to Tibet and become a monk, never to be heard from again? Right: you accept that you can't change the system, shrug, create lots of little shell companies, and open dollar accounts on sunny islands far, far away.
>
> I'm really not that bad. A victim of jealousy from time to time. But definitely no hypocrite.

Mohsin Hamid, *Moth Smoke*

Procedure

1 In class explain to students that you will now give them a second text, somewhat related to the first. Allow them about 15 minutes to read it silently and individually.

2 Working in pairs, they compare the two texts, noting all the similarities and differences they can find. These can relate to the theme (corruption), to the nature of the dialogue, to actual language items, to the setting, etc.

3 Pairs report back in a general discussion session. This should lead on to a more specific discussion of the theme of corruption, ethical behaviour, etc.

Variation

One week before the class, hand out the first text to one half of the class, and the second text to the other half. On the day the class takes place, pair up students who had the first text with those who had the second text. They then look for comparisons as above.

Sample text 2

> Martins said, 'Have you ever visited the children's hospital? Have you seen any of the victims?'
>
> Harry took a look at the toy landscape below and came away from the door. 'I never feel quite safe in these things,' he said. He felt the back of the door with his hand, as though he were afraid it might fly open and launch him into that iron-ribbed space. 'Victims?' he asked. 'Don't be melodramatic Rollo. Look down there,' he went on, pointing through the window at the people moving like black flies at the base of the wheel. 'Would you really feel any pity if one of those dots stopped moving—for ever? If I said you can have twenty thousand pounds for every dot that stops, would you really, old man, tell me to keep my money—without hesitation? Or would you calculate how many dots you could afford to spare? Free of income tax, old man. Free of income tax.' He gave his boyish conspiratorial smile. 'It's the only way to save nowadays.'
>
> 'Couldn't you have stuck to tyres?'
>
> 'Like Cooler? No, I've always been ambitious.'
>
> 'You are finished now. The police know everything.'
>
> 'But they can't catch me, Rollo, you'll see. I'll pop up again. You can't keep a good man down.' ...
>
> He turned his back and leaned his face against the glass. One thrust ... 'How much do you earn a year with your Westerns, old man?'
>
> 'A thousand.'
>
> 'Taxed. I earn thirty thousand free. It's the fashion. In these days, old man, nobody thinks in terms of human beings. Governments don't, so why should we? They talk of the people and the proletariat, and I talk of the mugs. It's the same thing. They have their five-year plans and so have I.'
>
> 'You used to be a Catholic.'
>
> 'Oh, I still believe, old man. In God and mercy and all that. I'm not hurting anyone's soul by what I do. The dead are happier dead. They don't miss much here, poor devils,' he added with that odd touch of genuine pity, as the car reached the platform and the faces of the doomed-to-be-victims, the tired pleasure-hoping Sunday faces, peered in at them. 'I could cut you in, you know. It would be useful. I have no one left in the Inner City.'

Graham Greene, *The Third Man and The Fallen Idol*

5.8 Book reviews and reports

Level All levels

Time 30 minutes to introduce the topic, plus homework

Aims To help students evaluate critically what they read; to develop the skill of writing a review.

Preparation

1 Print out one or two shortish reviews of some recent publications, perhaps of a novel and a professional book. (See 'Useful websites', page 126 for sites related to Activities 5.8 and 5.9.)

2 Make enough copies of the reviews for one per pair of students.

3 If you think it would be helpful, prepare a list of the elements a good book review should have.

Example **Book reviews**

1 An introduction which puts the book in context; and maybe something about the author, previous books on the same theme, how topical it is, etc.

2 A brief description of the contents or the storyline, so that readers know what it is about.

3 Some specific comments detailing plus and minus points.

4 A general evaluation/recommendation.

Procedure

1 Hold a brief discussion on book reviews. What is their function? How many of the students read them? How useful are they?

2 Students work in pairs to list the kind of information they feel a book review should provide. Allow ten minutes for this.

3 Collect feedback, then distribute your own list of points along with a sample review you chose. How far does the sample review conform to your prototype review list?

4 As a homework assignment ask students to write a review (not longer than 500 words) either of a novel they have read recently in English or of a professional book. In writing it, they should follow the guidelines discussed. Set a date for submission of the reviews, and schedule a class when students can exchange their reviews and comment on them.

Comments

The need to write a considered critical opinion about a book ensures that it is read with great care.

5.9 Deciding what to read

Level   All levels

Time   30 minutes to introduce the idea, plus follow-up

Aims   To help students develop a feeling for what they might want to read; to help them work out a reading plan.

Preparation

1   Make copies of some recent short book reviews which have interested you personally.

2   Print out a list of websites which offer information on recent books. (See 'Useful websites', page 126.)

Procedure

1   Initiate a discussion with students about what kinds of material they read. Here are some possible prompt questions:

- *How do you get to know about what you want to read?*
- *How do you decide to read one thing rather than another?*
- *When you pick up a book, how do you know whether you want to read it or not?*
- *How do you locate the parts of a book or article you want to read, discarding the rest?*

2   In pairs, students devise a checklist of strategies for selecting reading material (using reviews, websites, word-of-mouth recommendations, etc.), deciding whether a particular book or article is worth reading, or which parts of it are worth reading (checking the back-cover copy, the list of contents, random sampling of a few pages, etc.).

3   Collect suggestions in a general feedback session.

4   For homework, ask students to prepare a reading plan for the coming two weeks. Then monitor progress.

Comments

1   There is so much printed material available, not to mention online text, that we need to develop critical discrimination about what we read. This includes deciding to stop reading something if it is useless, boring, or does not fulfil our expectations of it. This saves us time and maximizes the benefits of what we read.

2   Developing a reading plan helps keep us on track, though plans are there to be changed too!

3   If you are studying independently, you can still do the activity. You will find ample material on the websites listed in 'Useful websites', page 126 under Activity 5.9.

5.10 Close reading

Level All levels

Time 60 minutes, plus follow-up

Aims To introduce students to textual features which tie the text together.

Preparation

Make copies of a text which is tightly organized and uses a number of cohesive and other discourse features. Here are two examples, though almost any text will do, since any text has to use such features to qualify as a text at all.

Sample text 1

> Imagine a piece of land twenty miles long and twenty miles wide. Picture it wild, occupied by animals small and large. Now imagine a compact group of sixty human beings camping in the middle of this landscape. Try to see yourself sitting there, as a member of this tiny tribe, with the landscape, your landscape, spreading all around you farther than you can see. No one apart from your tribe uses this vast space. It is your exclusive home-range, your tribal hunting ground. Every so often the men in your tribe set out in pursuit of prey. The women gather fruit and berries. The children play noisily around the camp site, imitating the hunting techniques of the men. If the tribe is successful and swells in size, a splinter group will set off to colonize a new territory. Little by little the species will spread. Imagine a piece of land twenty miles long and twenty miles wide. Picture it civilized, inhabited by machines and buildings. Now visualize a compact group of six million human beings camping in the middle of this territory. See yourself sitting there, with the complexity of the huge city spreading out all around you, farther than you can see.
> Now compare these two pictures.

Desmond Morris, *The Human Zoo*

Sample text 2

> **There are many ways to change the world**
> **Find yours**
> The world changes when people have the imagination to dream, and the strength to act. Martin Luther King had both. Our dream is of a world without poverty. To make it come true, we need to share, not just what we have, but what we know.
> Volunteer with VSO, and share your knowledge and your experience. Pass them on to others, who will pass them on, and on, and on. You will start a chain reaction, like Martin Luther King, and you will change the world. We urgently need experienced professionals, especially in health, education and business, to share their skills and change lives.
> **Find your way to change the world**
> **Volunteer with VSO**

Procedure

1 Explain that it can sometimes be useful to look more closely at a text to see how it hangs together. Ask for suggestions about how texts are connected internally, so that they form an intricate and tightly-woven fabric of threads. For example, there is always a system of reference backwards and forwards, usually by using pronouns to refer to nouns. There is also a system of lexical strings, that is, words which are in some way equivalent and which remind us of what the main ideas are. The text may even refer to things outside itself to tie it to ideological or other concepts.

2 Distribute your chosen text. Allow about ten minutes for students to read it carefully.

3 In pairs, or working alone if they prefer, ask students to note all the ways the text is tied together—through reference, lexical strings, comparisons, references to things outside the text, etc. Allow 15 minutes for this.

4 Collect ideas and comments in open session. Below are some of the points which should be made (The examples refer to the text of the VSO advertisement.).

Reference
- 'Find yours': your way to change the world
- 'King had both': both the imagination to dream and the strength to act
- 'make it come true': our dream
- 'Pass them on': your knowledge and experience

Ellipsis
- 'like Martin Luther King': (as he) did

Lexical strings related to themes:
- change: 'Change the World', 'changes', 'change lives'
- the world: 'The world', 'a world'
- dream: 'imagination to dream', 'Our dream', 'make it come true'
- sharing: 'need to share', 'share their skills'
- knowledge: 'what we know', 'knowledge and your experience', 'experienced professionals', 'share their skills'

Exo-textual reference
- 'Martin Luther King': I have a dream.

Note too the changes of pronouns between paragraphs:
- Title: 'Find yours' (you)
- Paragraph 1: 'people' (they), 'our dream' (we/us)
- Paragraph 2: 'Your', 'you', 'We'
- End title: 'Find your way' (you)

5 You might wish to discuss what the purpose of the text is (advertisement to persuade people to volunteer with VSO) and how this is linked to the repetition of the key themes in the lexical strings.

6 Distribute a second text for them to analyse as an assignment. Let this form the basis of the next class.

Comments

1 This kind of close reading is not 'reading' in its normal and natural sense. It is more akin to textual analysis. However, an awareness of how texts hang together can help us process texts more efficiently and enhance our appreciation of the skill with which they were constructed. It can also indirectly feed back into our own writing.

2 If you are working independently, you can follow exactly the same outline. Read the text carefully, then look at the sample analysis in Procedure step 4 above. Then choose your own text to work on.

5.11 Favourite poems

Level All levels

Time 60 minutes, plus follow-up

Aims To stimulate students' interest in poetry in English; to start a personal collection of favourite poems; to learn some poems by heart.

Preparation

1 Explain to students that as part of broadening their reading experience, and in preparation for 6.2 'Writing poems', they will look at a number of short poems, and perhaps re-evaluate their views on poetry.

2 Select about six poems in English that you are personally fond of, and prepare enough copies for one per student. The poems should preferably not be too long. It is easy to find suitable poems by doing an Internet search for the author or title. (See also 'Useful websites', page 126.)

3 Three of my personal favourites are Robert Frost's 'Acquainted with the Night', Shakespeare's 'Sonnet 73', and 'Tarantella' by Hilaire Belloc. You will naturally have your own favourites.

Procedure

1 Ask students about their experience of poetry. Here are a few prompt questions:
   - *How many of you read poetry (in English or in your own language)?*
   - *Do any of you remember a poem that you could recite by heart?*
   - *What use are poems?*
   - *What can they do that other kinds of text cannot?*
   - *Can it be useful to remember them by heart?*
   - *Why do you think that might be?*

2 Hand out the poems you have selected. Allow about 15 minutes for students to read them through.

3 In pairs, they then have to agree on the poem they like best. If they absolutely cannot agree, let them choose one each.

4 In class feedback, students share their choices, and then read them aloud.

Follow-up

1 As a follow-up project, encourage students to create a small collection of their own favourite short poems. Suggest anthologies they might look at. They could begin by trying some poems from the 'Further reading' list on page 123.

2 Students could also try some of the better-known websites. (See 'Useful websites', page 126.)

3 Encourage students to commit at least some of these poems to memory. Conduct a follow-up class where they can share their selections, and recite, (not read) their favourite poem(s).

Comments

1 Advanced learners can gain many advantages from reading poetry. They will discover language being used in creative ways. They will develop a sense of the underlying rhythms—the heartbeat—of the language, especially if they say the poems aloud or commit them to memory. In addition, they will have a store of delight they can draw on at any time.

2 Learning by rote is not fashionable in our times. However, if we can choose what to learn by heart, and if it is aesthetically pleasing, it will have value. Recalling favourite lines can be a great comfort at times, as well as a valuable support for language learning.

3 If you are working independently, you can still do the activity. Think about your possible answers to the questions in Procedure step 1. Then browse through some of the books and websites listed in 'Useful websites', page 126 and decide if poetry is for you!

6

Focus on writing

Advanced learners will usually need to be able to write a wide variety of text types. They will need to write accurately and appropriately, and sometimes to produce written text under time pressure. Above all, they will need to write for real purposes, whether these are professional or personal. To do this, they will need to take charge of their own writing. This is a formidable task, which even native speakers of a language often find difficult. The activities proposed in this chapter offer a range of writing tasks, and encourage the development of a writing habit through writing journals and letters.

6.1 Keeping a journal

Level All levels

Time 25 minutes for discussion, 25 minutes to write a sample entry, plus feedback

Aims To encourage students to adopt a regular writing habit; to develop freedom to explore facts, ideas, and feelings in a non-judgemental context.

Preparation

1 Ask students to bring a plain, new notebook to this class.

2 If you keep your own journal, photocopy a sample page for each student. A sample you can use if you do not wish to use your own appears on page 82.

Procedure

1 Introduce the notion of a personal journal, something like this:

This is a notebook in which you write something regularly, preferably every day, however little. A journal is more than just a diary. It is not simply a record of your day, such as 'Got up at 7. Had a shower and cooked pancakes for breakfast. Missed the train to London …', etc. In your journal, you can write about anything that interests you—books you have read, television or films you have watched, conversations you have had, ideas you have thought about, problems which are bothering you, dreams you have had, plans you are making, ideas for stories or poems, recollections of things that happened in the past, jokes you have heard—anything and everything. But you need only write about things which are really significant for you. There is no need to write about anything you don't feel is important. Also, there is no need to pay too much attention to correcting or editing for grammar or punctuation. The main focus is on the content. It is your journal—no one else's.

2 Hand out your sample journal page and allow students time to read it through.

3 Tell them they have 15–20 minutes to write the first entry in their new journal. The main thing is to write, not to worry about correctness. They will not be asked to show what they have written and it will certainly not be graded.

4 Allow 5–10 minutes for feedback on their writing. Ask what they wrote about, what difficulties they experienced, if any, and how they felt about the activity.

5 Ask them to set aside 30 minutes at the end of each day for writing their journal. Tell them that you will check that they have written regularly in two weeks' time, and reassure them that you will simply ask to see how much they have written, not what they have written.

Sample text

What a day again! I had so many plans and they all went out of the window because of constant interruptions—the plumber came (after keeping us waiting for two weeks!) and I couldn't ask him to come back another day… he'd never have been seen again. Then Nanny called. She has gallstones and has an op. next week. By then it was coffee time. I was just settling down to my review of Luke's book when the phone went again. My brother wanting to talk about what we do with the land my Dad left us in his Will … and so on. Before I knew it, it was lunchtime! It all reminded me of how we always seem to allow the immediate to get in the way of what is really important.

I had a funny dream last night. I was in the sea looking back at the coast. Some people were using some illegal fishing equipment but near me I saw a fishing line going down into the water. As I watched, a mermaid came out holding four fish on her hand. It gave me an idea for a story … must make some notes later before I go to sleep and forget it all.

Bad weather again. Pouring rain and the river is rising again. Flood warnings. I worry constantly now about global warming and climate change. We'll all be either under the sea or living in a desert soon, unless we've been blown away by a tornado or something before that.

Comments

1 Note that 1.4 'Keeping a study journal' and 1.5 'Keeping a language notebook/file' also offer opportunities for writing practice.

2 Some students may wish to show you their journals. Others will be fiercely private about them. Accept both reactions. It is certainly enlightening to read their journals if they wish it, as you will get a lot of informal feedback on many aspects of their progress.

3 The key things about a personal journal are that it is personal, and that it is not an exercise in accuracy. The main thing is to form the habit of writing regularly about something interesting.

4 If you are working independently, you can still keep a journal. It will help you get into the habit of writing regularly.

6.2 Writing poems

Level All levels

Time 60 minutes, followed by private writing time

Aims To stimulate students' creative use of language; to increase motivation through successful creative writing.

Preparation

1 Find an extract from a novel or short story with some colourful or striking words and phrases in it.

2 Make enough copies of your extract for one per student.

Sample text

> But when she woke up that morning, stirred out of sleep by a tiny housefly with gauzy wings and a pert black body, hopelessly lost, vagrant and restless, humming and hovering above her face, Akhila felt within her a queer itinerant sensation. An aftermath of her dream the night before, she thought.
>
> The fly settled on her brow for a fleeting second and rubbed its legs briskly. Flies did this all the time; loading and unloading disease and despair. But this one, new adult, had nothing to unburden but germs of disquiet. Akhila flicked the fly off with a sweep of her arm but the fly had accomplished what it set out to do. A snarl of maggot-like notions swam through the redness of blood and thought till Akhila felt a great desire to board a train. To leave. To go somewhere that wasn't landlocked like this city of Bangalore. To the end of the world, perhaps. Her world, at least. Kanyakumari.

Anita Nair, *Ladies' Coupe*

Procedure

1 Ask if anyone has ever written a poem before, either in English or in their own language. Elicit opinions about writing poetry. Some will be negative, but not all. Ask them to suspend judgement till they have written a poem in English.

2 Distribute the text you have prepared and ask them to read it through. They should then select ten words and/or phrases they find particularly striking, and write them down on a separate sheet of paper.

3 Collect back the sheets of the extract. Students now have their own sheet with ten words and phrases they have chosen. Tell them they are now going to write a short poem using the words and phrases on their paper. They may add other words too, of course. Their poem

does not have to rhyme, and they should not try to reconstruct the meaning of the Sample text, but simply let the words they have chosen suggest a meaning and a direction for their poem. You should also take part by writing your own poem.

4 Allow 15 minutes for writing. Students then work in pairs, reading their partner's poem. They may need to ask questions about what the poem means, or make suggestions for improvement.

5 In the final ten minutes of the class, ask if any students are willing to share their poems by reading them aloud. If there is any reticence, read your own poem first.

6 If students agree, publish their poems as a wall display, a booklet, or on a class webpage.

Comments

1 Many people have negative feelings towards poetry in general. It is also not uncommon for students to feel that writing poetry in a foreign language is simply 'too difficult'. It is the aim of this activity and many others like it, to demonstrate that writing poetry in a foreign language is not only possible, but curiously liberating.

2 For many other activities, see Jane Spiro, *Creative Poetry Writing* in this series. There are literally hundreds of techniques for stimulating creative poetry writing. This one is just one example.

3 If you are working independently, you might like to post your poem(s) on your blog to share them with others.

6.3 Writing a short story

Level All levels

Time 60 minutes, plus follow-up

Aims To activate students' story-telling potential; to submit the narrative urge to the discipline of length-constraint.

Preparation

Print out enough copies of a mini-saga for one per student. (A mini-saga is a story told in exactly 50 words.) Here is an example:

Sample text

> Little Red Riding Hood took food to Granny but Wolf had eaten Granny and sat in her bed. 'You look strange, Granny,' she said, 'those big ears … and those big teeth!' 'All the better to eat you with,' roared Wolf, leaping out of bed. But she had a pistol! Bang!

Alan Maley

Procedure

1 Conduct a brief discussion about stories. Try to get the message across that everyone has interesting stories to tell. Also, that stories are an important part of being human, and for transmitting knowledge and

wisdom. Find out if any of the students have written stories, in English or in their own language. If so, ask them to talk about their stories.

2 Tell students that there are many ways of getting started on writing stories. (See Follow-up below.) But today they will be writing a story 50 words long. They decide whether this will be a story about their own life, or a story they have heard, or know well, such as a folk story. Allow ten minutes for them to think and jot down the outline of their story.

3 Allow another 20 minutes for them to try to reduce their story to just 50 words. Then get them to exchange stories with a partner, who will try to suggest ways of shortening the story if necessary.

4 The homework assignment is to complete the mini-saga in time for the next class. Use part of that class time to check on the work and hear the stories read aloud by their authors.

Follow-up

Conduct other story-writing sessions. You will find many ideas in Jane Spiro's *Storybuilding* in this series. However, you do not need special techniques to write a story. All that is needed is a good strong plot or storyline, well described characters, interesting settings, and some lively dialogue.

Comments

1 Stories really are the stuff of life. When students begin to tell their stories there is a qualitative difference in the classroom atmosphere. Students also begin to 'discover their voice' in the foreign language and there is a significant growth in self-esteem and confidence.

2 If the story-writing catches on, make sure to publish the stories. Students will take a great deal of care in the way they present their stories visually if they know they will be published. They will also gain enormous confidence in the process.

3 If you are working independently, try to publish what you write on a blog or website so that you can be in touch with others who share your writing interests.

6.4 Writing 'real' letters

Level All levels

Time 60 minutes, plus follow-up

Aims To give students experience in writing letters to real people and organizations on real issues.

Preparation

Make a list of some key issues—international, national, and local, for example, the abolition of land mines, the question of immigration into other countries, the case against landfills in the local area.

Procedure

1 Many people feel powerless in a world where important decisions always seem to be taken without much consultation with those whose lives will be most affected by them. Discuss with students how they can have some kind of impact on such decisions. One way, which will emerge, is to write letters as part of campaigns to affect decisions or to express personal views. Ask for the names of organizations which have done or are doing this. For example, Amnesty International, Oxfam, Action Aid, etc.

2 Working in groups of three, students compile lists of issues—at least one international, one national, and one local. Allow about ten minutes for this.

3 Collect the information and list the issues on the board in three columns: *International   National   Local*

Students then decide on just one issue they would like the class to address. The issue should be very clear-cut so that everyone understands exactly what it is, and what they want to do about it. Students then go back into their groups and brainstorm the organizations or institutions they plan to write to. For example, the names of national or local newspapers, NGOs like Oxfam, CARE, foreign embassies, local government offices, ministries or government departments. After about ten minutes, let them regroup and share this information.

4 Set groups an assignment to a) research the issue b) decide on which organizations or individuals will receive the letters, and c) make a first draft of the letter they propose to send.

5 In the following class, groups report back on their assignment. They compare drafts of their letters and decide on an agreed, edited version from each group. You will need to check on the accuracy and appropriacy of the final drafts. The class then sends the letters to the agreed recipients.

Follow-up

With any luck you should have at least a few replies, which can be used as input to a new round of letters. Keep a file of the letters students send, the names of the institutions, and the replies, where relevant. This will be useful for future groups of students to consult.

Comments

1 The motivation for writing is greatly increased if the students know their letters are about something important and will actually be read by someone.

2 For many other ideas on using letter-writing, see Burbridge et al., *Letters*, and Sampedro and Hillyard, *Global Issues*, also in this series.

3 If you are working independently, you can still do the activity but you will not have the help of a group, so you will need to research everything yourself.

6.5 Email discussion groups

Level All levels

Time 60 minutes to set up, plus follow-up

Aims To involve students in regular and focused use of email; to remind them of the rules of 'netiquette'.

Preparation

You will need to set up a discussion group online. One way to do this is to:

- Go to a search engine homepage. Click on 'groups'.
- On the next page, click on 'start a group'.
- You will then be asked to sign in with your username and password. If you have not got one, you will need to apply for one.
- There are three steps to setting up a group:
  Step 1: Choose a category (schools/education). Click on it and choose from the menu of options (classmates).
  Step 2: Enter a name (top.advanced@) and a group email address (group.co.uk), for example. Then write a brief description of the group's activities in the box provided.
  Step 3: You're on!

Procedure

1 Tell students that you have set up an email discussion group site for them. This will make it easy for everyone to share information as well as to discuss topics decided by the group. Incidentally, it will give them opportunities for a lot of writing practice.

2 Decide on a possible topic for the first round of discussions. Make sure everyone knows what it is. Then give them the group address. Tell them that you will post an introductory message on the topic. They will then be free to respond. Ask them to log on at least once a day in order to keep up with the discussion and to contribute to it.

3 Set some ground rules after discussion with students. For example:

- no 'flaming' (expressions of anger)
- not too much personal banter
- no self-exclusion—all members of the group should contribute, etc.

Students may wish to add more.

4 Set some time aside in the following week to review progress and possibly decide on new topics. You will need to do this regularly.

Comments

1 One issue which may arise is the style of writing in emails. Email is a hybrid form, with many features of speech expressed in written form. You will need group consensus on how informal the style should be. Some groups may wish to stick to a more formal written style. Others may prefer the informality of abbreviations, rebuses, and smilies characteristic of personal emails.

2 The email discussion group is a very effective way of getting regular writing practice. It also contributes to the formation of group solidarity.

3 If you are working independently, you can join an existing group by choosing one from the menu when you check the Yahoo groups website.

Acknowledgements

I am indebted to Chris Lima for her advice on setting up discussion groups.

6.6 Writing job applications

Level All levels

Time 60 minutes, plus follow-up

Aims To help students write better job applications; to give practice in writing them.

Preparation

Collect a number of job advertisements from your students' professional fields. If possible, ask them to bring in advertisements which would be of interest to them.

Procedure

1 Discuss the importance of the way a letter of application for a job is written. What do students think are the most important issues? After a few minutes' discussion, write up these criteria on the board:

Accuracy   Appropriacy   Clarity   Economy   Elegance

2 In pairs, students discuss what might be meant by these criteria.

3 Explain, if necessary, what the terms refer to:

- Accuracy: This means that the information provided is accurate, and that the language is also accurate—spelling, grammar, choice of vocabulary.
- Appropriacy: Is this information relevant to the job description? Are there details which you do not need to mention? Is the tone appropriate (not too aggressive/not too subservient)? Is the language at the right level of formality?
- Clarity: Is the letter absolutely clear in its expression? Are there any ambiguities or instances of confusion, repetition, poorly chosen vocabulary? Is the structure of the letter clear and logical?
- Economy: Does the letter say just enough but no more? Or does it include too much information which clutters up the message, and gets in the way of the main points?
- Elegance: Does it leave the reader feeling that it was 'a good read'? That everything about it was aesthetically well balanced?

4 Ask students to choose one of the job advertisements they or you have brought to class. They then write the first draft of a letter applying for the job. Allow about 15 minutes for this.

5 They exchange their drafts with a partner. Partners edit the drafts they have received, then discuss the changes they have made.

6 Students take away their drafts and revise them before the next class. In that class, discuss as many of the drafts as possible in detail.

Comments

1 It would be tempting to provide a model letter for this activity. However, given the many various types of job specifications, this would not be helpful. It is preferable to work on the application letters on a case-by-case basis.

2 If are working independently, you can still do the activity, but it will work best if you have a 'study-buddy' who can offer you feedback.

6.7 Abstracts and biodata statements

Level All levels, but mainly high advanced

Time 60 minutes, plus follow-up

Aims To give students practice in writing to length in an appropriate genre.

Preparation

1 You will need to find a conference 'Call for papers' which specifies what prospective speakers have to supply by way of an abstract and biodata. This information will obviously vary according to the professional field in question. An example is shown below.

2 Make enough copies of your text for one per student.

Sample text

> ### Abstract
> Your abstract should be 200–250 words long. The title should be no longer than ten words. The abstract must make clear your purpose and point of view. State the structure of the presentation, the evidence and the findings, and the way in which your presentation is relevant to the theme of the conference.

Biodata

A brief 150-word maximum biodata statement which mentions your professional achievements, current research interests, and publications.

Procedure

1 Check how many students have already had to prepare abstracts and biodata statements for professional conferences, symposia, or seminars. Use whatever experience they have had to feed in to the activity. Students decide on the theme of the conference they will be attending. They then draft an abstract and a biodata statement to fit the conference theme. Allow about 30 minutes for this.

2 Students work in pairs. They exchange their abstracts and biodata and make suggestions for improvements.

3 Collect the edited abstracts at the end of the class. Use them as input for the next class, when you can discuss their effectiveness.

4 If you are working independently, you can do the activity by following the Sample text instructions and asking a sympathetic friend to check your abstract and biodata.

7

Focus on listening

Spoken language can be 'understood' at different levels: recognition, where the words of the message can be decoded; comprehension, where the message is understood on a factual level; and interpretation, where the significance of the message, including the subtext, is fully understood. Clearly, at an advanced level it is interpretation skills which need to be developed, and interpretation implies critical listening. As we listen, we constantly evaluate critically what we hear. And this holds for whatever type of listening we do: transactional, interactional, or aesthetic. A further dimension of listening at this level is the ability to process non-standard varieties of English. Finally, the advanced learner develops a greater sensitivity to voice quality and tone. The activities in this chapter focus therefore on the quality of listening.

7.1 Fast dictation

Level All levels

Time 30 minutes, repeated regularly

Aims To develop students' ability to understand language spoken at normal speed; to draw on all language resources to reconstitute a text accurately.

Preparation

1 Select a short piece of prose or poetry within the proficiency level of the students.

2 Make enough copies of your text for one per student.

3 The Sample text below would be suitable for medium advanced level.

Sample text

> It was a room designed to impress visitors, with framed photographs of Keith with the President of the Republic, Keith with the Queen, Keith with the Minister of Trade and Industry. The bookshelves were lined with the latest books on management, and a state-of-the-art personal computer stood on his desk.

Alan Maley, *He Knows Too Much*

Procedure

1 Inform students you will give them a dictation—but not in the usual slow way. You will read the text at normal speed. Tell them that the first time you read it, they should not write anything, just listen. When you finish, they write down anything they can recall: words, phrases, etc. The second time you read it they write as you read, trying to fill in gaps. The third time, they try to complete the text. Tell them that after the third reading you will give them time to confer with their classmates till they are satisfied they have the original text accurately transcribed.

2 Read the text at normal speed. Students listen but do not write. As soon as you finish, they write whatever they can recall.

3 Read it again at normal speed. This time they can write as you read.

4 Read it a third time. This time they try to fill in all the gaps so that they have a complete text.

5 Now tell them to work with one or more partners, to compare their versions and decide on a final, correct version.

6 Distribute the text and allow time for them to compare their versions with the original. Encourage discussion of any differences they note.

Variation

With basic advanced students, distribute the text first. Allow just five minutes for them to read it. Then collect the texts. After that proceed as above.

Follow-up

This is an activity you should do regularly. It will take less time as you do it more frequently. You can progressively hand over responsibility to the students. Encourage a student to take over the reading, and ask the class to bring you texts which could be used in future.

Comments

1 This activity provides repetition in a motivated context. It also calls upon the total language repertoire of a learner (phonological, lexical, and grammatical) in the attempt to reconstitute the text.

2 If you are studying independently, you can do the activity differently. Choose a text at random. Read it aloud once, quickly. Then put it away. Write down what you can remember. Read it again quickly then put it away again. Write what you can recall. Do this three times. Then compare your version with the original. If you cheat, you are only cheating yourself!

7.2 Analysing interviews

Level   All levels

Time   60 minutes, plus follow-up

Aims   To raise students' awareness of verbal strategies used by participants in television interviews; to develop a critical sense when viewing media events.

Preparation

1   Students will need to watch a recorded television interview. For long interviews, see the BBC World series *Hard Talk*. For shorter examples, see some of the interviews on a quality news programme. A good example in the UK is the BBC's *Newsnight*. The interviews should preferably cover a controversial topic or event.

2   You may also want to prepare a short checklist of items you want students to look out for.

3   Make enough copies of Worksheet 7.2 for one per student.

Worksheet 7.2
Checklist for interviews

1   What types of question does the interviewer use?
2   Does the interviewee always answer the question?
3   If not, what do they do instead? For example, do they answer a question with another question? Do they evade the question by slightly changing the subject? Do they answer a different question? Do they simply ignore the question?
4   How often do the speakers interrupt each other?
5   How do the speakers 'hold the floor', i.e. how do they manage to continue speaking even when the other speaker is trying to get a word in?
6   How aggressive is the interviewer?
7   Does the interviewee talk down to the interviewer by using phrases like, 'No. What you've got to understand is … ', 'I think you underestimate the complexity of … ', 'That's not the point at all.' 'I don't think you've been listening to me'?
8   Is the interviewee ever at a loss for words?
9   Does the interviewee use jargon phrases like, 'at the end of the day … ', 'to be perfectly honest with you,' 'in my experience …', 'be that as it may … ', etc?

Photocopiable © Oxford University Press

Procedure

1   Discuss the types of interviews, usually on current affairs, which we often see on international or national television channels. In many cases these interviews involve a more or less confrontational situation. The interviewer sees it as his/her duty to make the interviewee admit things which might be damaging. The interviewee

seeks to avoid giving straight answers to the questions, to divert the interview into safer areas, or to get across a message the interviewer does not want to hear. How do they achieve this? Hold a brief discussion on behaviours students have noticed in interviews.

2 Distribute Worksheet 7.2. Allow a few minutes for students to digest it, then ask if there are any points they would like to add. Explain that they will now watch an interview and use the worksheet to make notes.

3 Play the interview once to allow students to get the gist of it. Then play it again, this time pausing every minute or so to allow students time to make notes. Finally play it through again so that students can check any points they may have missed.

4 In a feedback session, collect the points which students noted under each of the worksheet items. Here are a few prompt questions you could ask:

- *Have you learnt anything about the 'interview game' played daily on screens across the world?*
- *If you had been the interviewer, would you have done things differently? How?*
- *What advice would you offer to the interviewee?*

Variation

This activity can also be done outside class, either in the self-access centre or at home. In this case, students use Worksheet 7.2 to write a brief report which they then present in class.

Comments

The deviousness of politicians is legendary. They are not merely 'economical with the truth' but evade questions, even when they have no real need to. (See, Peter Oborne, *The Rise of Political Lying* for well documented examples.) As advanced users of English, it is important for students to develop critical listening skills. This activity will help them not only not to believe everything they hear, but to understand why they should not!

7.3 Transcriptions

Level All levels

Time 20 minutes to introduce the idea, plus written assignment

Aims To give students training in listening for detail.

Preparation

1 Record a two-minute radio news bulletin or news reportage.

2 Make a transcription by writing out what the news item said.

3 Make enough copies of your transcription for one per student.

Procedure

1 Distribute the copies of the transcription and play the newscast from which it was taken. Students read it alongside the recorded version.

2 Explain that a transcription must be a completely accurate written record of the spoken version.

3 As a homework assignment, ask students to make their own recordings of a news bulletin. They then make an accurate transcription to hand in with their recordings. Note that the recordings should be erased as soon as the transcriptions have been checked for accuracy.

Comments

1 The activity obliges students to listen very intensely and repeatedly. This is excellent listening training for other contexts.

2 If you are working independently, this is an ideal activity for you. If you cannot get hold of recordings from real radio stations, make your own news broadcast and record that.

7.4 Subtitles

Level All levels

Time 30 minutes to introduce the idea, plus follow-up

Aims To develop students' ear for spoken dialogue on film or video.

Preparation

You will need to prepare a film clip of about three minutes' duration, with plenty of dialogue.

Procedure

1 Introduce the topic of films. Here are some suggestions for prompt questions:

- *How much cinema do you watch?*
- *What are your favourite films or types of film?*
- *How do you think deaf people manage to enjoy films?*

One way is to provide subtitles.

2 Show the film clip twice, then show it a third time. This time, allocate different students to different characters. As they watch, they should try to record in writing what their character says.

3 Check on what they have written. Then play the clip again so they can check for themselves.

4 As a homework assignment, ask each student to choose their own film clip to work on. Set a deadline by which they must submit their clip and the subtitles.

Comments

Dialogue in films is not always easy to understand even for native speakers of English. This activity is valuable in that it requires intensive and repeated exposure to recorded sound.

7.5 Selective listening

Level Medium and high advanced

Time 60 minutes

Aims To develop students' ability to focus on selected aspects of listening; to report on these aspects.

Preparation

1 You need to have access to a few minutes' recording from a radio or television interview.

2 Alternatively, you could record an informal discussion between two of your teacher-colleagues on a recent event or incident (with their permission, of course!).

Procedure

1 Before the listening begins, allocate different tasks to different students (or pairs or groups). Here are some ideas of the kinds of examples of language they should listen for:

- vague language (*sort of, you know what I mean, like, you see*)
- figurative language
- 'mistakes', where the speaker corrects himself/herself
- false starts, where the speaker has to go back and start again
- interruptions
- question types used. (*Don't you think …?* versus *Do you think …?*)

2 Explain that they will be listening to (or viewing) part of an interview. As students listen, their attention will be focused only on the item they have been allocated. They will be the 'specialist' in that particular conversational feature.

3 Play the recorded extract once or twice so that students get the gist of what the topic is. Check on any comprehension problems at this point.

4 Play the recording again. This time, they focus on their special feature, making notes as they listen. Repeat this at least three times.

5 Students take turns to report back on what they noted for their feature. Where necessary, replay the parts of the extract to verify their notes.

Variation

This activity can be done out of class, provided students have access to a recording. Alternatively, they can make their own recorded extracts. They then note down all the features listed and bring the recording and analysis to class for discussion. This has the advantage of allowing them to listen to the extract as many times as they need.

7.6 Notes and questions

Level All levels

Time 60 minutes, repeated at intervals

Aims To develop students' critical listening capability; to practise
formulating critical questions about what they hear.

Preparation

Either prepare a recorded version of a short current affairs speech
or prepare a short speech yourself based on a current issue. In
either case, the topic should be controversial, for example, the case
for voluntary euthanasia; the need for higher taxes on big, petrol-
guzzling cars; the case for nuclear power stations, etc. The talk
should last no longer than about ten minutes.

Procedure

1 Explain to students that they will hear a short speech on a controversial
topic. As they listen to it, they should formulate some written questions
to clarify the points being made or to challenge them.

2 Play or give the talk. Students then work in pairs to formulate
their questions. Allow about ten minutes for this. Then collect the
questions in a feedback session.

3 If there is time, students could role-play speaker and questioners so
that the 'speaker' would have to respond to the questions.

Variation

1 As a homework assignment students formulate questions on a
number of current affairs issues. They could either brainstorm the
issues in class or you could supply a list.

2 They would then need about a week to make themselves thoroughly
familiar with their chosen issue before formulating their questions.

3 On the due date, a group of students form a 'panel of experts' with a
chairperson. The assignment questions would be put from the floor,
with the panel having to respond. This is the format of the successful
BBC radio programme *Any Questions?* Though it is not exclusively a
listening activity, listening is an important part of it.

7.7 Listening triangles

Level All levels

Time 30–40 minutes

Aims To develop students' listening and reporting skills; to practise
interview techniques.

Preparation

Prepare a list of simple interview topics. For example:
- favourite dishes in your country
- education in your country

- your favourite writer/artist/singer/actor
- your future career plans
- grandparents
- bringing up children.

Procedure

1 Divide the class into groups of three. Explain that student A will interview student B for five to ten minutes. Student C takes careful notes in order to be able to formulate questions and comments.

2 Write the topics on the board and allow the groups to choose a topic each. All the student As will be interviewers. They will need about five minutes to jot down some questions. The student Bs will be the interviewees, and the student Cs, the note-takers. All students should use the five minutes to anticipate what questions might be asked.

3 The groups conduct the interviews, followed by feedback from the Cs. They may come up with questions like *I wonder why you didn't mention …? Perhaps you could have asked a bit more about … .*

4 In full-class feedback, suggest some of the question types which are useful for eliciting information from interviewees. For example:

- *Perhaps we could start by talking about … .*
- *So, when did you first …?*
- *Oh. That's interesting. Could you tell me a bit more about that?*
- *I wonder if you ever considered …?*
- *I've often wondered why … . Could you explain that to me?*
- *I totally agree with you there, but don't you think …?*

Elicit further suggestions from the class.

5 Groups then reassemble and choose a different topic. This time the Bs interview the Cs, and the As take notes. Tell students to try to incorporate at least some of the listed questioning gambits into the interviews.

6 After open feedback, groups choose a third topic. The Cs interview the As, while the Bs take notes. By the end of the class, each student will have played all three roles and covered three different topics.

Follow-up

Repeat this activity a few lessons later. This time students will have more time to think about the topic. They should prepare questions in advance, and practise them through 'inner speech' rehearsal. This means, they 'hear' themselves asking the questions in their head without speaking them aloud. This is a powerful way of getting practice and can be done anywhere—on the bus, in the shower, or sitting in a café.

Comments

1 This is an excellent activity for encouraging really careful listening. The comments from the reporter are very important in helping to improve the quality of the questions and the responses.

2 If you are working independently, you cannot do this activity as it is. However, you can engage with it differently. Choose a topic, and write out some questions. Think of how you would ask the questions and do some 'inner speech' rehearsal. Then record the questions (speak them, don't read them), leaving space on the tape for answers. A few days later, play the tape and answer your own questions.

7.8 He talks funny …

Level All levels, especially high advanced

Time 60 minutes, plus follow-up

Aims To expose students to a wide range of accents; to stimulate thought and debate on how English is used in the world; to increase awareness of attitudes to accents.

Preparation

1 You will need a recording of about ten different English accents. There is a very convenient collection in Andy Kirkpatrick, *World Englishes*. This has a CD and transcripts of the recordings. (See 'Further reading', page 123.)

2 If you are really keen, consult J. C. Wells, *The Accents of English*. Alternatively, if you have access to a number of native speakers of English from different countries, try making your own recording with them.

3 Prepare enough copies of Worksheet 7.8 for one per student.

Worksheet 7.8
The accent

Circle your answer to each question.

(1 = quite easy 5 = incomprehensible)

1 How easy was it to understand?

| Easy | 1 2 3 4 5 | Difficult |

2–9 How did it sound?

2 Musical	1 2 3 4 5	Harsh
3 Educated	1 2 3 4 5	Uneducated
4 Pleasant	1 2 3 4 5	Unpleasant
5 Funny	1 2 3 4 5	Irritating
6 Nice person	1 2 3 4 5	Not a nice person
7 I'd like to sound like this.	1 2 3 4 5	I wouldn't like to sound like this.
8 Correct English	1 2 3 4 5	Incorrect English
9 Clear-sounding	1 2 3 4 5	Foggy-sounding

Procedure

1 Lead a discussion about accents in general. Here are some suggestions for prompt questions:

- *How many different regional accents are there in your own language?*
- *What is your attitude to these accents?*
- *How are they regarded in your country (educated/uneducated, socially acceptable/unacceptable)?*
- *How about attitudes to different English accents?*
- *How many of these accents have you heard before?*
- *How easy were they to understand?*
- *How about your own speech? Do you have an accent in English?*
- *How do native English speakers react to it?*

2 Distribute Worksheet 7.8. Explain that you are going to play some extracts of different accents in English. After each one, students should note what they feel, using the checklist headings. Play the first extract, allowing time for them to make notes. Then play the next extract. Do this for the first five extracts. Then play them all again, one after the other, so that they can refresh their auditory memory.

3 Check their responses in a class feedback session. How different were their reactions? Lead the discussion around to attitudes to accents. Remind them that perceptions of accents are highly subjective—it is only other people who have accents, never us!

4 Discuss what often happens in practice when two people with rather different accents meet: they usually modify their speech to something closer to their interlocutor. This is called 'accommodation'.

5 If there is time, play a few more accents. Ask *Did you find it easier this time?*

Comments

1 It is important for students to realize that they will meet a wide variety of accents in English. They need to be prepared for this, and to develop a tolerance for this variety. They also need to be aware of their own accents and consider how they can make themselves more easily comprehensible to others.

2 You may wish to discuss students' attitudes to native-speaker English. It may have come as a surprise to them that native speakers also have a wide range of accents, some more appreciated than others. Some advanced students would like to sound 'like a native speaker'. Ask students *Is this a realistic goal? How important is it to retain your own accent in English as a symbol of your identity?*

3 This activity also raises the question for students *What is a native speaker?*

7.9 Who's best?

Level All levels

Time 30 minutes

Aims To sharpen students' perception of voice qualities; to stimulate reflection on their own vocal qualities and how they might be improved.

Preparation

You will need to make a recording of about five people all reading the same short text. Almost any text will do. Make sure that the speakers have rather different ways of speaking. If possible have a mix of female and male voices, young and old voices.

Procedure

1 Explain that you will be playing a recording with different speakers all reading the same text. As they listen, they need to grade the speakers on a scale of 1–5 (1 being the lowest score, 5 the highest) on the following criteria:

- Clarity: How clearly does the speaker enunciate the words?
- Speed: Is it too fast? Too slow? Just about right?
- Pausing: Are there enough pauses? Are they the right length?
- Volume: Too loud or too soft?
- Modulation: Good rhythm and pace?
- Tone/mood: Warm/Cold? Bright/Dark?
- Accent: Too strong? Not attractive? Fine?

2 Write these criteria on the board or print them if it is easier. Before you play the recording, remind students that they should give answers for themselves. There are no right answers—everyone perceives things subjectively.

3 Then play the recording, with pauses between each speaker to allow time for students to note their perceptions.

4 Collect their impressions. Ask them:

- *How much difference was there between your evaluations of the different voices?*
- *What have you learnt about the way people judge others' voices?*
- *Would you do anything to change any of these aspects of your own voices? For example, by speaking more slowly, paying more attention to pauses, and to the affective tone of your voice?*

5 See also Activity 8.6 'Who is my model?'

8
Focus on speaking

Advanced learners may wish to improve their speaking skills in one or more of the following ways: by becoming more fluent, more expressive, more persuasive, more confident, more native-like, or by developing speaking skills related to their professional lives. Personal aspirations will largely shape what any individual decides to focus on. What is certain is that we are immediately evaluated on the basis not only of what we say but of how we say it. Our voice is as individual and unique as our fingerprints, and in a competitive world, where professionals are often called upon to speak in public, how they sound can be a critical factor. In this chapter, therefore, some activities focus on voice quality and expressivity, others on presentation skills.

8.1 Changing moods

Level All levels

Time 30 minutes, repeated at intervals

Aims To encourage students to express mood and feeling through voice quality; to interpret it in others; to extend the expressive qualities and range of their voices.

Preparation

Choose and print out a set of sentences or short texts which offer scope for multiple interpretations.

Sample text 1

> 1 Time and tide wait for no man, you know.
> 2 That was the last I saw of him.
> 3 And it was his 80th birthday too.
> 4 I told him it was probably better to leave things like that for the time being.
> 5 And she thought bungy-jumping was fun.

Sample text 2

> You came. You were late. As usual. But you came. It was a rainy day. But you came. And sunshine filled the world. And music filled the world. Though it was raining. And grey.

Leon Leszek Szkutnik, *Thinking in English*

Sample text 3

> The fields stretched away flat to the horizon. It was dawn. Ben stood at the bedroom window, Karen's cup of tea in his hand. He wondered if he should mention the smoke to her.

Alan Maley, from 'No Smoking'

Procedure

1 Take a sentence and demonstrate how it could be read with many different mood colours: happy, overjoyed, depressed, disappointed.

2 Write these words on the board:

Angry	*Nervous*	*Unhappy/tearful*
Disappointed	*Impatient*	*Depressed*
Optimistic/cheerful	*Humorous*	*Confidential*

3 Students work in groups of three. Distribute the short texts you have chosen. Students take it in turns to read the texts, using one of the mood words for their interpretation. The other two students in the group have to guess which mood is being expressed.

4 In a feedback session check on any problems or issues that arose. Suggest that this is something they could do outside class, either alone or with a friend.

Variation

Do the same activity using single words, rather than texts or sentences. For example: *Hello. Who? Now. Never. Love. True. Well.* Students say these single words with a particular situation in mind and the others must try to guess the situation or context: Where is it taking place? Who is speaking to whom? About what? Why?

Comments

Everyone has a tendency to fall into vocal habits when they speak. Some people always sound rather low key and flat, others sound bubbly and excited. This activity is one way of breaking out of vocal habits and exploring a wider range of the voice.

8.2 Who am I?

Level All levels

Time 60 minutes, plus follow-up

Aims To focus students' attention on the 'presentation of self'; to give practice in some basic presentation skills; to develop confidence in public speaking.

Preparation

1 If you decide to do Variation 2, collect together various items such as: a stone, a piece of driftwood, a coin, a foreign postage stamp, a banknote, a fountain pen, a watch, a mobile phone, a credit card.

2 A week before this class, ask students to prepare a 2–3 minute talk to introduce themselves to the rest of the group. Their aim is to make the talk as interesting as possible—to present themselves as an interesting person to know! They should include two unusual facts about themselves, one true, one false! For example, *I worked in a gold mine once. I have a collection of 18th century surgical instruments.*

Procedure

1 On the day of the class, students take it in turns to give their presentations. The others need to keep notes and grade the presentations from 1–5 under these simple headings:

Interest   Clarity of speech   Clarity of information   Confidence
They also need to note which fact they thought was true and which false.

2 During open feedback, students vote on the evaluation scores and check on the true and false facts. Which students were the winners?

Variation 1

Rather than presenting themselves, they can talk about someone they know well or have strong feelings (positive or negative) about.

Variation 2

Distribute a number of common objects you have collected to students before the class: a stone, a piece of driftwood, a coin, a foreign postage stamp, a banknote, a fountain pen, a watch, a mobile phone, a credit card, etc. They then prepare to present themselves in role as the object they have been allocated. They do this verbally, but can act out their object as well if they wish.

Follow-up

After the first presentation session, ask students to prepare to redo their initial presentations in the light of their first experience and the feedback they received. This time, all the information they give should be true.

8.3 Presentation skills

Level All levels

Time 2 class hours, repeated as necessary

Aims To develop students' skills to a high standard for public presentations; to raise awareness of the effects of poor presentation skills; to offer practice in making and critiquing presentations.

Preparation

1 Prepare enough copies of Worksheet 8.3 for one per student.

Worksheet 8.3
Evaluation form for presentations

Characteristics	Grade (1–5)	Comments
Content	_____	_____
Clear purpose	_____	_____
Organization	_____	_____
Density of information	_____	_____
Relevance to audience	_____	_____
Use of relevant examples	_____	_____
Use of transitions	_____	_____
Clarity	_____	_____
Pacing/timing	_____	_____
Visuals: quality	_____	_____
Visuals: use	_____	_____
Audience rapport	_____	_____
Eye contact	_____	_____
Voice:	_____	_____
• Volume	_____	_____
• Speed	_____	_____
• Tone	_____	_____
• Pronunciation	_____	_____
Gestures/body language	_____	_____
• Hand gestures	_____	_____
• Facial expressions	_____	_____
• Posture	_____	_____
Use of space	_____	_____
Handling of visuals	_____	_____
Other	_____	_____

2   Make a list of possible presentation topics for students to choose from. Here are a few possible examples, but many others may be more relevant to your particular group:

- my education
- career planning
- my favourite author/musician/actor
- the future of the world
- food and its effects.

Procedure

1   Conduct a general discussion about the effectiveness of presentations to a public audience. Here are some possible leading questions to start off with. List these on the board:

- *What kinds of presentations are you familiar with?*
- *Can you think of a particularly successful one (either one you attended or gave)?*
- *How important is it to you to be able to present in public in English?*
- *How often do you/will you need make presentations?*
- *What do you think are the most important factors in a successful presentation?*

2   Distribute Worksheet 8.3. How does it compare with the items you have collected from the students and written on the board? Are there any important points they raised which are not in the checklist? If so, add them to the worksheet under 'Other'.

3   Go through the evaluation form with them, explaining any items which they are not familiar with. For example, *Transitions*, which means the devices the speaker uses to get smoothly from one point to another—phrases like 'Moving on to my next point …', 'By contrast, the …', etc.

4   Allocate one presentation topic to each student. Alternatively, they can choose from your list, or come up with topics more relevant to their own interests or purposes. They then prepare a ten-minute presentation for a future class.

5   In that class, students take turns in making their presentations. Their classmates complete the checklist (and so do you!) and offer feedback and suggestions for improvement. If at all feasible, make video recordings of at least some of the presentations and use them for the feedback sessions (and for future instructional purposes, provided you obtain the subjects' permission to do so).

Comments

1   Most students at this level will be well aware of the importance of making public presentations in English (or in their own language) and many will have experience of making them. The amount of information and discussion will depend on the level of experience and sophistication of the group. There is no point in wasting time on lengthy explanations to experienced business people, for example. On the other hand, it is important to offer them an analytic framework for planning and evaluating presentations.

2 This is obviously not a one-off activity. It should be repeated as often as needed, and may even form a regular part of an advanced course.

3 If you are working independently, this will be more difficult for you to do. However, you could consider persuading a friend to complete the checklist for you. Alternatively, you could be videoed and complete the form as a self-evaluation.

8.4 Readers' theatre

Level All levels, with appropriate text level

Time 60 minutes, with repeat performances at intervals

Aims To develop students' text interpretation skills; to encourage ensemble skills.

Preparation

Select one or more short texts. Poems are best but extracts from short stories or even advertisements may be suitable for some groups. Make enough copies for one per student. Here is an example:

Sample text

> **Living**
>
> I am the grass
> I am the tree.
> And I am you.
> And you are me.
>
> I am the earth.
> I am the sun.
> And I am you,
> And we are one.
>
> I am the air.
> I am the sea.
> And I am you.
> And you are me.
>
> I am the ocean.
> I am the weather.
> And you and me
> Must stick together.
>
> I am the sand.
> I am the granite.
> We're all connected
> On this planet.
>
> I am the earthquake, the typhoon.
> I am the dark side of the moon.
>
> I am the drought.
> I am the flood.
> I am the sickness
> In our blood.
>
> I am in everything
> And so are you.
> So what can we,
> Together, do?

Alan Maley

Procedure

1 Spend about ten minutes explaining the task. Students will work in groups of about six. Each group is to prepare an orchestrated performance of their text in which they all have a part to play. It adds to the interest if each group has a different text. Groups must try to make the text as interesting to listen to as possible. Explain how they can do this—by pausing, varying speed, volume, pitch level; by adding sound effects or gestures and movement; or by varying the number of speakers of different parts of the text. Deal with any questions at this point.

2 Divide the class into groups of five or six. Distribute the texts. Allow 20 minutes' preparation and rehearsal time. Monitor the groups discreetly as they work.

3 Each group performs their text. The other groups then provide feedback on what they liked most about the performance and suggestions for improving it.

4 Tell the groups that they will all have the chance to perform their text again at the beginning of the next class.

Variation

You may choose to do step 1 of the Procedure in one class, then ask the groups to prepare and rehearse outside class. The performance is then given in the next class.

Comments

1 The benefits of working on a text in this way are enormous. Students learn to work together. They come to a deeper understanding of the text from the commitment of working on it from the inside, rather than from the viewpoint of a dispassionate reader. They take great care (and pride) in rehearsing a polished performance, with a commensurate increase in motivation.

2 It is well worth making this activity a regular part of your classes. Students should be encouraged to take over more responsibility, for example in the choice of texts, etc. They may even wish to organize a public performance.

8.5 Doing it better

Level All levels

Time 60 minutes, plus follow-up

Aims To encourage students to give and take evaluative feedback; to use feedback to improve presentation skills.

Preparation

The week before this class divide the students into groups of three. Each group chooses and prepares two topics to discuss. Or you can assign topics if you prefer. Here are a few suggestions:

- It is too late to save the world from catastrophe.
- How can we ensure that wealth is more evenly distributed globally?
- Sport leads to damaging forms of aggression.
- Life is sacred, so there is never any justification for killing.

Procedure

1 On the day of the class, students work in groups of three to discuss the topics they chose previously. Students A and B discuss the topic for five to ten minutes. As they discuss, Student C takes notes on the effectiveness of their arguments, the language they use, the tone of the discussion, etc.

2 Student C then gives feedback to A and B. They then rerun the discussion incorporating the suggestions.

3 Student C then discusses the second topic with B, while A takes notes. Finally, students A and C discuss either topic while B takes notes.

Follow-up

If possible, students should record a debate on a given topic from a radio or television discussion programme. After listening to the various arguments, they could prepare their own contribution to present in class, going back over and improving the points made in the discussion. This is an invaluable way of honing both the arguments themselves and the language used to frame them.

Comments

If you are working individually, you may wish to use the suggestion in Follow-up above. This will give you useful listening practice, and will also provide ideas for your own contribution. If possible, exchange your contributions with a 'study-buddy' who is willing to give you feedback.

8.6 Who is my model?

Level All levels

Time 20 minutes to introduce the idea, plus follow-up

Aims To alert students to the possibility of basing their voice on a model speaker; to raise awareness of how they sound to others.

Preparation

If possible, prepare a recording or CD of a number of well known voices: television news readers, politicians, public 'personalities', actors.

Procedure

1 Lead a class discussion on voice quality. Here are some suggestions for prompt questions:

- *What kinds of voices do you find attractive to listen to?*
- *What is it that makes a voice attractive or unattractive to you?*
- *Are some kinds of voices always unpleasant to listen to?*
- *How do you react to nasal or adenoidal voices, throaty, thrusting voices that seem to attack the listener, boring, monotonal voices that lack energy, creaky voices, very high-pitched, screeching voices?*

2 Students then discuss together in fours to come up with a description of the kind of voice they think would be best for them. They may wish to illustrate this by comparing it with a well known public figure.

Questions for students to consider might include:

- *How much does accent matter?*
- *Is it better to try to sound like a 'native speaker' or like a well educated 'non-native speaker'? Why?*
- *What do like most about your own voice? And least?*

3 Collect feedback from the discussions. Are there any agreed features they would like to incorporate into their voices?

4 If you have a recording of some well known voices, play it and discuss how attractive or otherwise students find the different voices.

5 Suggest that over the coming two weeks, they listen more carefully than usual to all the voices they hear using English. They might like to pick one which they could model their own voice on.

Comments

1 Many successful users of foreign languages report that they find it helpful to model their own way of speaking on that of a particular user of that language. Equally, there are many people who find this unhelpful, and who regard doing this as a kind of invasion of their personality. Be aware of this when carrying out the activity. If there are students who do not wish to model themselves on another speaker, respect that. However, even for these students there is a lot to be gained by an enhanced awareness of voice quality and the effect it has on listeners.

2 If you are working independently, this may be a very helpful activity for you. In the absence of a teacher, a voice model may help you acquire the kind of English voice you want.

9

Focus on culture

Culture and language are inextricably intertwined. Yet it proves extremely difficult to define precisely what culture is. And even if we were able to define it, it is doubtful whether culture as such would be teachable. However, it is undeniable that an awareness of culture and cultural differences is an essential part of an advanced proficiency in using a language. Students at this level also need to be aware of the fast-changing and hybrid nature of culture in an increasingly globalized world. The focus in this chapter then, is not to try to teach culture but rather to encourage learners to engage with the realities of cultural difference, with how it operates, and how it intersects with language.

9.1 So what is culture?

Level All levels

Time 60 minutes

Aims To raise students' awareness of the many components of culture; to encourage them to reflect on aspects of their own culture.

Preparation

1 Make enough copies of Worksheet 9.1a for one per student.

2 Make copies of a concordance line for 'culture'. Alternatively or additionally, make enough copies of Worksheet 9.1b for one per student.

> ... a masculine occupational **culture** and quickly identified as ...
> ... of the most sophisticated **culture** in the Ancient Near East ...
> ... the popular (and vague) **culture** there are hundreds of ...
> ... expedition to soak up **culture** in London's East End ...
> ... of the Phoenicians, whose **culture** dominated fifth-century Ashkelon ...
> ... of research in material **culture** studies declined and tended ...
> ... the moment of mass **culture** yielding to pop culture ...
> ... substratum such as tissue **culture** plastic, the cells attach ...
> ... to show, the political **culture** remains predominantly an allegiant ...
> ... dictionaries of Language and **Culture** not only for literary ...
> ... human beings of a particular **culture** behave in such a ...

Worksheet 9.1a

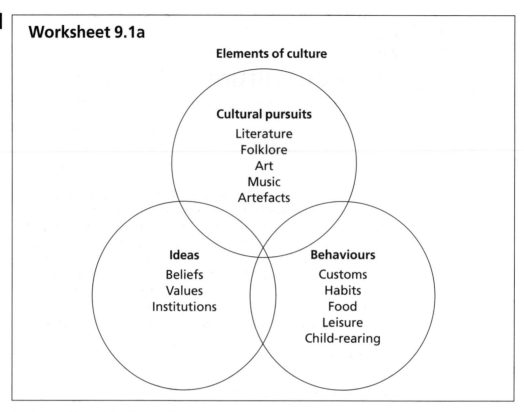

Elements of culture

Cultural pursuits
Literature
Folklore
Art
Music
Artefacts

Ideas
Beliefs
Values
Institutions

Behaviours
Customs
Habits
Food
Leisure
Child-rearing

Procedure

1 Lead a discussion on the meaning of 'culture'. Ask students:
   - *How do we recognize a culture?*
   - *What are the elements that make up a culture?*
   - *How important is culture?*
   - *How are language and culture related?*
   - *Can we learn a language without becoming involved in its culture?*
   - *Do all members of a recognizable group share the same culture?*

   Take about 15 minutes over this, and let the discussion be as wide-ranging as possible.

2 Distribute Worksheet 9.1a. Students work individually and note down specific elements of their own culture which match the categories. For example, under food, they might note 'vegetarian' or 'no alcohol', or 'pasta/pizza'. Allow 15 minutes for this.

3 Students share their findings with a partner, looking for commonalities and differences.

4 Conduct a full-class feedback session. Ask:
   - *What key factors emerged when you compared your cultures?*
   - *What additional light do they shed on the meanings we associate with culture?*

Worksheet 9.1b

Words commonly found in association with 'culture'

- barbaric culture
- bar-room culture
- boardroom culture
- Chinese/French/Hindu culture
- criminal culture
- culture of abuse
- culture of addiction
- culture of consumption
- culture of dependency
- culture of inequality
- culture of neglect
- culture of secrecy
- culture of violence
- drug culture
- educational culture
- feminist culture
- gun culture
- high culture
- hip hop culture
- indigenous culture
- Iron Age culture
- knife culture
- local culture
- locker-room culture
- medical culture
- musical culture
- national culture
- peasant culture
- popular culture
- smoking culture
- street culture
- sustainable culture
- teenage culture
- tribal culture
- visual culture
- working-class culture
- youth culture

Follow-up

1 Then distribute Worksheet 9.1b and/or the concordance line. As a homework assignment, ask students to collect the collocations which follow the word 'cultural' from newspapers, the Internet (cultural concepts, cultural differences, cultural diplomacy). In a future class, discuss what further light these cast on the notion of culture.

2 Set a written assignment on the topic: *Cultural stereotypes: advantages and dangers*. It is important to emphasize that stereotypes can be very useful, because they offer a framework of expectations for dealing with the complexity of a new situation; but they can also be a handicap if we use them to prejudge people from a different culture before we have even met them. There are a number of helpful websites on the subject. (See 'Useful websites', page 126.)

Comments

1 Culture is a word used so frequently now that it has almost lost any real meaning. This activity is intended to stir up the many interpretations which we unthinkingly give to culture, and to open our minds to the possibilities for human contact that 'culture' offers.

2 One way of thinking about culture is to consider it in the context of a 'family resemblance'. This is a concept proposed by the philosopher Wittgenstein. He applied it to many complex but ill-defined concepts, like games. When a concept has a family resemblance, it shares a large number of characteristics, but not all of these are found in every particular case. With culture, we may find a French person who eats baguettes (so do English people these days!), speaks a non-standard variety of French, drives a Peugeot, drinks pastis, reads *Charlie Hebdo*, hates J. P. Sartre, doesn't like cheese, etc. Some of these

things are supposed to be typically (stereotypically) French, others are not. In other words, we share many things in our culture with others—but not all of them. Hence the danger of stereotyping.

3 If you are working independently, think about the answers you might give to the questions in Procedure step 1, complete Worksheet 9.1a, and decide how important culture is to you in your language learning.

9.2 A day in the life of …

Level All levels

Time 60 minutes

Aims To raise students' awareness of the way culture affects everyday events; to compare the patterning of events in the everyday lives of people from different cultures.

Preparation

One week before you conduct this class, set students the task of recording the things they do in their own culture in any typical day throughout the day until they go to bed, for example, what time they get up, their ablutions, morning greetings, rituals, breakfast, what they eat, whether they eat alone or with the family, transportation to work or school, etc.

Procedure

1 On the day of the class, students work in groups of three and exchange their information. If they are from different cultures, this will be interesting. But even if they are all from the same culture, it will also throw up some interesting differences within a single culture.

2 The groups then merge and re-form so that students are working with different classmates. After a brief exchange of information about their typical days, they should compare their days with their experience (or preconceived ideas) about a day in the life of someone from British, American, Australian, or New Zealand culture. How different are they?

3 In full-class feedback, collect some of the issues that arose. How 'typical' is typical? How easy was it to compare their own life patterns with others from the same culture? Or with what they perceive as patterns in a different, 'foreign' culture?

9.3 Objects

Level   All levels

Time   60 minutes

Aims   To alert students to the atmospheric power of 'things' in their own and others' cultures.

Preparation

One week before this class, ask students to reflect on the kinds of objects that surround them in their home culture. If possible, they should also bring in pictures to illustrate what their world looks like. Below are some examples of questions they might reflect on:

- *In your room, what is the furniture like? The decorations? The size and shape of windows? The floor and any coverings? What personal things do you value?*
- *The bathroom? The kitchen area? The utensils used for cooking? Food storage?*
- *Your home: how big is it? What materials are used? Typical appearance? What are the colours? What is the garden area like?*
- *The appearance of streets around you: are they wide, narrow, straight, winding? What are the road surfaces, paths, and sidewalks like?*
- *What does the 'street furniture' consist of? (things like post boxes, telephone booths, taxis, buses, petrol stations, shops, walls and gates, vegetation, monuments, public buildings, banks, schools, post offices, notices and signs) What are their shapes, size, colours, etc?*
- *Describe restaurants and other food outlets.*
- *What about people's appearance: clothing, hairstyles, way of walking, facial expressions, way of talking?*

Procedure

1   On the day of the class, allow about 15 minutes for students to exchange their information in threes.

2   Then collect feedback from the whole class, item by item. Ask questions such as:

- *What differences emerge from this?*
- *How important are 'things' in our cultures and in our lives?*
- *Is globalization causing our living spaces to look more and more alike?*
- *What do you think are the most significant visual aspects of the English-language cultures you are familiar with?*

Comments

1   'Things' are the most superficial aspect of our cultures yet they nonetheless exert a powerful influence on how we feel and act.

2   If you are working independently, consider how the personal objects around you reflect your culture and how different they may be from any English-language culture you are familiar with.

9.4 What we believe and how we behave

Level All levels

Time 60 minutes, plus follow-up

Aims To raise students' awareness of what different cultural beliefs and behaviours have in common; to reflect on how they are different.

Preparation

1 Print out enough copies of Worksheet 9.4 for one per student.

2 One week before this class, distribute Worksheet 9.4. and ask students to prepare to respond to the issues raised.

Worksheet 9.4

How important are the following in your culture?

1 What do people in your culture believe in relation to these items? And how do they behave?

- The family?
- Marriage?
- Friendship?
- Love?
- Child-rearing?
- Status of men and women?
- Old age?
- Poverty?
- Religious belief?

- Politics?
- Ethical behaviour?
- Sickness and death?
- Ambition?
- Education?
- Teachers?
- Money?
- Crime and punishment?

2 Is there general agreement in your culture about these views and beliefs, or is there a wide variety of opinions?

3 Is there a difference between what people are supposed to believe and what they actually believe?

Photocopiable © Oxford University Press

Procedure

1 On the day of the class, students spend about 15 minutes in pairs comparing notes on their responses to the questions.

2 In open session, lead the discussion of these issues. It does not matter if you cannot cover all of them. (See Variation.) The important thing is to encourage an in-depth, probing discussion. Encourage them also to compare the beliefs in their own cultures with those in an English-speaking culture.

Variation

In one class, ask students to brainstorm a list of items related to cultural beliefs and values. Then allocate two or three items to groups of three students. In the following class, they present their items to the rest of the class, followed by discussion. The presentations can extend over two classes if necessary.

Comments

1 Beliefs and values are part of people's deep identity, so they are usually strongly defended. You can therefore expect some lively debate. You may feel that some items are too sensitive to include. However, beliefs are at the heart of culture, and if the students are mature and articulate, there is no point in avoiding issues just because they are sensitive. Avoidance will not lead to better understanding. But this is clearly a decision you, the teacher, must make in the context of your own class situation. (See Barry Tomalin and Susan Stempleski, *Cultural Awareness*, also in this series, for more activities on this theme.)

2 If you are working independently, you may wish to do this as a written activity, where you compare your own beliefs with those of an English- speaking country. Alternatively, try to discuss the issues with a friend by email correspondence.

9.5 It really gets on my nerves

Level All levels

Time 60 minutes

Aims To raise students' awareness of things which cause irritation in cross-cultural contexts; to discuss these negative behavioural factors in order to defuse tensions.

Procedure

1 Briefly introduce the issue of behaviours which irritate us. Elicit a few examples, such as people who leave a room and do not switch off the light, people who say, 'you must come round sometime' and then never invite us, people who eat with their mouth open, etc.

2 In pairs students brainstorm at least five things they find irritating about the English-speaking culture they know best, or in which they are living. Allow about 20 minutes for this.

3 Hold a feedback session where students share their irritations, and discuss possible reasons behind these behaviours. How similar are the sources of irritation? Explore possible ways of dealing with them.

Follow-up

If you can obtain a video or DVD of *The Joy Luck Club*, show a clip from the scene where the American fiancé manages to offend his Chinese girlfriend's parents with his inappropriate behaviour during dinner.

Comments

It is often quite small things which irritate us about other people. However, if we are aware of the 'rules' of another culture, we can avoid giving unnecessary offence. (In some cultures, for example, it is the 'rule' that you take off your shoes before entering someone's home; that you do not touch a person's head; that you avoid blowing your nose in public, etc.).

It is much more difficult, however, to find tactful ways of letting other people know what you find irritating about their behaviour! At least in the context of the classroom, you can try to establish a non-judgemental and unthreatening atmosphere which will help open students' eyes to behaviours they had not realized might be irritating to others.

9.6 Whose fault was it?

Level All levels

Time 60 minutes

Aims To explore 'critical incidents' in cross-cultural encounters; to develop strategies for dealing with such incidents.

Preparation

1 Print out enough copies of Worksheet 9.6 describing 'critical incidents' for one per student.

Procedure

1 Make sure students understand what is meant by a 'critical incident'. Essentially this is an event where one or both participants feel uncomfortable or worse, because of a cultural misunderstanding.

2 Hand out Worksheet 9.6 and invite students to comment on any one of the incidents. Ask:

- *What went wrong?*
- *Was anyone to blame?*
- *What could have prevented the misunderstanding?*

3 Students now work in pairs. They try to recall an incident where they were involved in a similar kind of misunderstanding. What could have been done to prevent or to remedy the incident?

4 In class feedback, students share their stories and their understandings. Maybe remind them that for 'them', we are 'them'.

Comments

1 It is only natural for us to see the world through our own cultural spectacles. This makes us tend to think that our own behaviour is legitimate and reasonable and that of 'the other' is not. This may sometimes be absolutely true but more often the problem arises because we have failed to put ourselves in the shoes of 'the other'. This activity is designed to make students more aware of the relativity of cultural practices.

2 If you are working independently, you can still do this activity. Read the worksheet texts. Then think back to any incident where you remember feeling uncomfortable in an exchange with someone of another culture. Can you see what might have gone wrong? Is there anything you could have done about it?

Worksheet 9.6

Critical incidents

1 Ying is a young Thai student in the UK. In her culture it is polite to show respect to elders. One of her male teachers, in his 50s, invites her to his house for a party. She smiles a lot and seems to have accepted but she does not go to the party, because to her it seems like over-familiar behaviour. When the teacher sees her on Monday morning, he looks unfriendly and says to her, 'My wife was disappointed you did not come.' He does not invite her again.

2 Ha is a Vietnamese student in London. She loves writing stories in English, so when her school announces a competition for stories to appear in a publication, she is overjoyed. She shows one of her stories to her English friend Janice, who reads it and tells her it is very good. Ha is heartbroken when her story is not even shortlisted.

3 Jiang is a highly-motivated Chinese student of English at an Australian university. She is very keen to do well and often asks her Australian friends for advice or help. They usually agree. After about six months, she goes to a friend's room at about 11 p.m. to ask about some vocabulary in her essay. She is deeply hurt when her friend tells her to come back at a reasonable hour. She never asks this friend for help again.

4 Phuc is a university lecturer from Vietnam working in Australia. He goes to a conference in Malaysia. The conference organizer has booked a taxi for him at 4.30 a.m. so that he can catch his early return flight. He is a nervous traveller and the organizer has been very considerate, so he calls the organizer at 2 a.m. to make sure the taxi booking has been made. He is never invited to Malaysia again.

5 Brian (English) has been at a conference in China. The night before he is due to leave, his hosts present him with a large framed oil painting. There is no way he can carry it with him so he hides it on the top of the wardrobe in his hotel room and leaves it there. He is about to leave for the airport when a room maid appears in the lobby with the picture he has 'forgotten' in his room. His hosts are not amused.

9.7 How did they do things then?

Level All levels

Time 60 minutes, plus follow-up

Aims To show students how all cultures share certain key elements with varying emphases; to use other cultures to shed light on our own.

Preparation

1 Prepare enough copies of Worksheet 9.7 for one per student.

Worksheet 9.7

Cultural elements checklist

Products	Behaviours	Ideas/beliefs
Art	Customs (birth, initiation, death, marriage, etc.)	Institutions (law, government, education, etc.)
Music		
Language		
Literature (including oral literature)	Foods and drink	Family
	Leisure activities (sports, games, theatre, etc.)	Ethics
Clothing		Religion
Agriculture	Status of women	
Industry	Hierarchies	
Weapons	Taboos (on language, gestures, actions)	
Cult objects		
Buildings		

Photocopiable © Oxford University Press

Procedure

1 Explain that students will be carrying out a mini-project. Write on the board the names of some ancient cultures/civilizations. How much do students already know about these ancient civilizations?

Here are some suggestions:
Ancient Greece, Ashanti, Aztec, Chola, Dogon, Edo Japan, Maya, Khmer, Ottoman Turkey, Songhai, Tang Dynasty China, Vijayanagara, Zulu under Shaka.

2 In groups of three, students brainstorm a list of features which any culture would exhibit. If they have already done some of the other activities in this chapter, this should not take long. Allow about 15 minutes for this.

3 Hand out Worksheet 9.7. Ask students to compare what they brainstormed with the checklist in the worksheet. There may be some items of their own that they would like to add to it.

4 Set a deadline for presenting the project, which should be an in-depth study of the culture they have been assigned. You can decide whether to assign one culture per group or allow them to choose, or to do it as a lucky draw! They will need to research their culture on the Internet, where they will find more than enough material.

5 On the due date, groups present their findings, with supporting visuals or documentation as appropriate. What has the project taught them about 'culture' in general? Are there useful lessons to be learnt from the past?

List of sample text references

Chapter 3

Activity 3.1

The Oxford Dictionary of Collocations. 1991. Oxford: Oxford University Press

Oxford Collocations Dictionary for Students of English. 2009. Oxford: Oxford University Press

The Oxford Thesaurus. 1991. Oxford: Clarendon Press

Concordance lines from British National Corpus: www.natcorp.ox.ac.uk/index.xml

Activity 3.2

Nunan D. 2007. *What is this thing called language?* p.126. Basingstoke: Palgrave Macmillan.

Lawson, N. February 2008. *Time* magazine, p.45. Time Inc.

Activity 3.9

Maley, A. *The Best of Times?* 2008. Cambridge: Cambridge University Press.

Chapter 4

Activity 4.1

Maley, A. 1999. *He Knows Too Much*, p.76. Cambridge: Cambridge University Press.

Activity 4.3

Concordance lines from British National Corpus: www.natcorp.ox.ac.uk/index.xml

Activity 4.7

James, W. 1902. *The Varieties of Religious Experience*, pp. 170–171. Penguin: New York.

Chapter 5

Activity 5.3

Morris, D. 1967. *The Human Zoo*, p.1. London: Jonathan Cape.

Activity 5.6

Brontë, C. *Jane Eyre*. pp. 529–30. Edinburgh: Thomas Nelson.

Brontë, C. 1978. *Jane Eyre*. pp.141–2, Evelyn Atwell (ed.) Harlow: Longman,

Brontë, C. 2008. *Jane Eyre*, pp.96–7, retold by Clare West. Oxford Bookworms Library. Oxford: Oxford University Press

Activity 5.7

Hamid, M. 2000. *Moth Smoke* London: Granta Books.

Greene, G. 1977. *The Third Man*, pp.104–5, and *The Fallen Idol*, p.105–6, Penguin: New York.

Activity 5.10

Morris, D. 1967. *The Human Zoo*, p.1. London: Jonathan Cape.

VSO website: www.vso.org.

Chapter 6

Activity 6.2

Nair, A. 2001. *Ladies' Coupe*, p.3. London: Vintage Books.

Chapter 7

Activity 7.1

Maley, A. 1999. *He Knows Too Much*, p.23. Cambridge: Cambridge University Press.

Chapter 8

Activity 8.1

Szkutnik, L. L. 1984. *Thinking in English*, p.77. Warszawa: Panstwowe Wydawnectwo Naukowe.

Maley, A. 1997. 'No Smoking' from *Musical Cheers and other Short Stories*, p.30. London: Penguin.

Chapter 9

Activity 9.2

Concordance lines from British National Corpus: www.natcorp.ox.ac.uk/index.xml

Further reading

Chapter 1

Activity 1.1
Morrow, K. 2004. *Insights from the Common European Framework*. Oxford: Oxford University Press.

Activity 1.4
Goleman, D. 2006. *Social Intelligence*. Bantam Books.

Goleman, D. 1996. *Emotional Intelligence*. Bloomsbury Publishing.

Activity 1.5
Manser, M. H. and **D. Pickering.** 2007. *Buttering Parsnips, Twocking Chavs: The Secret Life of the English Language*. London: Weidenfeld & Nicolson.

Activity 1.6
Dictionaries
Oxford Advanced Learner's Dictionary. 2000. Oxford: Oxford University Press.

Cambridge International Dictionary of English. 1995. Cambridge: Cambridge University Press.

Longman Dictionary of Contemporary English. 1990. London: Longman.

Macmillan English Dictionary for Advanced Learners. 2002. Basingstoke: Macmillan.

The Longman Language Activator. 1993. Harlow: Longman.

The Longman Essential Activator. 1997. Harlow: Longman.

Specialized dictionaries
Oxford Collocations Dictionary for Students of English. 2009. Oxford: Oxford University Press.

Oxford Dictionary of Humorous Quotations. 2005. Oxford: Oxford University Press.

Brewer's Dictionary of Phrase and Fable (17th edition). 2005. London: Weidenfeld & Nicholson.

Penguin Dictionary of Abbreviations. 1989. London: Penguin.

Penguin Dictionary of Clichés. 2000. London: Penguin.

20th Century Words. 1999. John Ayto (ed.) Oxford: Oxford University Press.

Longman Dictionary of Contemporary English. 1987. Harlow: Longman

Rees. N. *A Word in your Shell-like: 6000 curious and everyday phrases explained*. 2006. London: Collins.

Grammars
Swan M. *Practical English Usage*. 1995. Oxford: Oxford University Press.

Cambridge Grammar of English. 2006. Cambridge: Cambridge University Press.

Collins Cobuild English Grammar. 1996. London: HarperCollins.

A Grammar of Contemporary English. 1972. Essex: Longman.

A Communicative Grammar of English. 2002. London: Pearson.

A University Grammar of English. 1974. Essex: Longman.

The Plain English Guide. 1996. Oxford: Oxford University Press.

Books about English
The Oxford Companion to the English Language. 1996. Oxford: Oxford University Press.

The English Language. 1990. London: Penguin.

The Story of English. 2002. Universität Paderborn.

Crystal, D. *The Stories of English*. 2004. New York: Overlook Press.

Activity 1.8
Krashen, S. 2004. *The Power of Reading: Insights from the Research*. Englewood, CO: Libraries Unlimited.

Activity 1.10
Donne, J. 1972. *Complete Poetry and Selected Prose*. London: Nonesuch Press.

Chapter 2

Activity 2.1
Crystal, D. 2005. *How Language Works*. London: Penguin.

Activity 2.2
Rudzka, B. 1993. *The Words You Need*. London: Macmillan.

Chapter 3

Activity 3.7
The Oxford Dictionary of Word Histories. 2004. Oxford: Oxford University Press.

Chapter 4

Activity 4.2
Biber, D., S. Conrad, and D. Leech. *A Student Grammar of Spoken and Written English*. 2002. London: Longman.

Carter, R. and M. McCarthy, *The Cambridge Grammar of English*. 2006. Cambridge: Cambridge University Press.

Activity 4.9
Swan, M. *Practical English Usage*. 1995. Oxford: Oxford University Press.

Chapter 5

Activity 5.1
Bamford, J. and R. R. Day. 2005. *Extensive Reading Activities for Teaching Language*. Cambridge: Cambridge University Press.

Activity 5.4
Furr, M. 2007. *Bookworms Club Reading Circles: Teacher's Guide*. Oxford: Oxford University Press.

Activity 5.11
Heaney, S. and T. Hughes (eds.). 1982. *The Rattle Bag*. London: Faber & Faber.

Jones, G. R. (ed.) 1996. *The Nation's Favourite Poems*. London: BBC Books.

Jones, G. R. (ed.) 1998. *The Nation's Favourite Comic Poems*. London: BBC Books.

Jones, G. R. (ed.) 1997. *The Nation's Favourite Love Poems*. London: BBC Books.

Benson, G., J. Chernaik, and C. Herbert (eds.) 1998. *Poems on the Underground*. London: Cassell.

Reid, C. (ed.) 1998. *Sounds Good: 101 Poems to be Heard*. London: Faber & Faber.

Hughes, T. (ed.) 1997. *By Heart: 101 Poems to Remember*. London: Faber & Faber.

Cope, W. (ed.) 1998. *The Funny Side: 101 Humorous Poems*. London: The Poetry Society.

Chapter 6

Activity 6.2
Spiro, J. 2004. *Creative Poetry Writing*. Oxford: Oxford University Press.

Activity 6.3
Dahl, R. 'Little Red Riding Hood' in *Revolting Rhymes*, London: Puffin Books. 2008.

Spiro, J. 2006. *Storybuilding*. Oxford: Oxford University Press.

Activity 6.4
Burbridge, N. et al., 1996. *Letters*. Oxford: Oxford University Press.

Sampedro, R. and S. Hillyard. 2005. *Global Issues*. Oxford: Oxford University Press.

Chapter 7

Activity 7.2
Oborne, P. 2005. *The Rise of Political Lying*. London: Free Press. 2005.

Activity 7.8
Kirkpatrick, A. 2007. *World Englishes*. Cambridge: Cambridge University Press.

Wells, J. C. 1982. *Accents of English*. Cambridge: Cambridge University Press.

Chapter 9

Activity 9.4
Tomalin, B. and S. Stempleski. 1993. *Cultural Awareness*. Oxford: Oxford University Press.

Useful websites

Chapter 1

These come with the usual 'health warning': they may disappear overnight, so it is worth starting your own list of sites you have found useful and to browse for more.

Activity 1.5

ruth@laraconsultancy.com.

Activity 1.7

www.mapmyword.com (via personalized Google)

www.teachingenglish.org.uk/think/think.shtml

www.blog-efl.blogspot.com

www.britannica.com (free *Encyclopaedia Britannica*)

www.dictionary.cambridge.org (Cambridge dictionaries online)

www.oup.co.uk/elt/oald (*Oxford Advanced Learner's Dictionary*)

www.lexfn.com (Lexical freenet)

www.ucl.ac.uk/internet-grammar/home.htm (*The Internet Grammar of English*)

www.edunet.com/english/grammar/index.cfm (*The online English Grammar*)

www.googleblog.blogspot.com (To create a Google blog: go to Google, click 'More', select 'Blogger', then follow instructions.)

www.dictionary.com (Dictionary.com)

www.answers.com (Answers.com)

www.worldwidewords.org (World Wide Words)

ww.wordspy.com (The Word Spy)

www.gutenberg.net/catalog (Project Gutenberg)

www.bbc.co.uk (BBC *Interactive*)

www.onestopenglish.com/ (Macmillan Onestop English)

www.cnn.com/transcripts (CNN Transcripts)

www.voanews.com (*Voice of America*)

www.bbc.co.uk/worldservice/learningenglish/ (*BBC Learning English*)

www.bized.ac.uk (Biz/Ed)

www.news.bbc.co.uk/sport (*BBC Sport*)

www.soccernet.com (*Soccernet*)

eviews.net/accentsinenglish.html (*E Views Accents in English*)

www.englishlistening.com (The English Listening Lounge)

www.realguide.real.com (Real.com Guide)

www.microsoft.com/uk/education/newsletter/archive

Chapter 2

Activity 2.2
dico.isc.cnrs.fr/dico/en/search *English Synonym Dictionary* (includes visual mapping of semantic fields)

www.e-synonym.info/ *Synonym Dictionary*

synonyms.memodata.com/ *Synonyms: free online English dictionary*

dictionary.reverso.net/english-synonyms/Collins *English Thesaurus*

Activity 2.5
www.ipl.org/div/subject/browse/ref32.00.00/ Ipl The Internet Public Library gives lists of free encyclopedias.

www.encyclopedia.com

encarta.msn.com/artcenter_/browse.html MSN Encarta

en.wikipedia.org/wiki/Main_Page

www.thefreedictionary.com

Chapter 3

Activity 3.1
www.natcorp.ox.ac.uk/index.xml

Activity 3.4
www.englishclub.com/vocabulary/prefixes.htm

en.wiktionary.org/wiki/Appendix:Suffixes:English

dictionary.reference.com/help/faq/language/t11.

www.learnenglish.org.uk/CET/flashactivities/suffixes02html

Activity 3.5
www.wordfocus.com

Activity 3.6
www.askoxford.com/worldofwords/newwords/?view=uk

www.teachingenglish.org/think/vocabulary/newwords.html

www.randomhouse.com/words/newwords/50_90s.html

Activity 3.7
en-wikipedia.org/wiki/listsof_English_words_of_international_origin

Chapter 4

Activity 4.3
www.natcorp.ox.ac.uk/index.xml

Activity 4.4
www.gray-area.org/Research/Ambig/

Activity 4.6
englishplus.com/grammar/mistcont.htm

andromeda.rutgers.edu/~jlynch/Writing/

esl.about.com/od/englishgrammar/English_Grammar_Help_Rules_Worksheets_Games_Quizzes_Exercises.htm

Chapter 5

Activity 5.2
www.vuw.ac.nz/lals/staff/paul-nation/nation.aspx.

Activity 5.8
www.reviewcentre.com
www.highbeam.com/landing/book_reviews.aspx

Activity 5.9
www.lovereading.co.uk
www.timesonline.co.uk/tol
www.reviewcentre.com/products1291.html
www.books.guardian.co.uk/reviews/

Activity 5.10
www.eliteskills.com/classics.php

Activity 5.11
www.tfl.gov.uk/tfl/corporate/projectsandschemes/artsmediadesign/poems/
plagiarist.com/
www.bartleby.com/verse

Chapter 6

Activity 6.5
uk.groups.yahoo.com

Chapter 7

Activity 7.8
collectbritain.co.uk/collections/dialects/
accent.gmu.edu/

Chapter 9

Activity 9.1
en.wikipedia.org/wiki/stereotype
www.newscientist.com/article.ns?=dn8111

Activity 9.2
www.natcorp.ox.ac.uk/index.xml

Index